From the ordinary to the extraordinary,

The
WINE-OH!

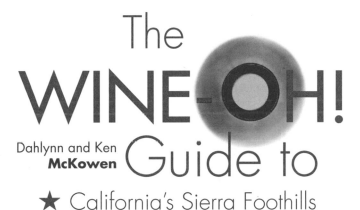

Dahlynn and Ken
McKowen Guide to

★ California's Sierra Foothills

Featuring wineries in Nevada, Placer, El Dorado,
Amador, and Calaveras counties

For
Carry & Ann
Cheers !
Ken McKowen
Dahlynn McKowen

🐾 **WILDERNESS PRESS** ... *on the trail since 1967*
BERKELEY, CA

The Wine-Oh! Guide to California's Sierra Foothills:
From the Ordinary to the Extraordinary

1st EDITION 2009
  2nd printing February 2010

Interior photos, except where noted, by the authors
Maps: Scott McGrew
Cover and book design: Steve Sullivan, STEVECO International
Book editors: Roslyn Bullas and Laura Shauger

ISBN 978-0-89997-492-7

Manufactured in Canada

Published by: **Wilderness Press**
                1345 8th Street
                Berkeley, CA 94710
                (800) 443-7227; FAX (510) 558-1696
                info@wildernesspress.com
                www.wildernesspress.com

Visit our website for a complete listing of our books and for ordering
information.

Cover photo courtesy of www.winepictures.co.uk

To Dahlynn's parents,
Scharre and Cliff Johnson:
Because we know you both appreciate
the finer things in life,
including a great box of wine!

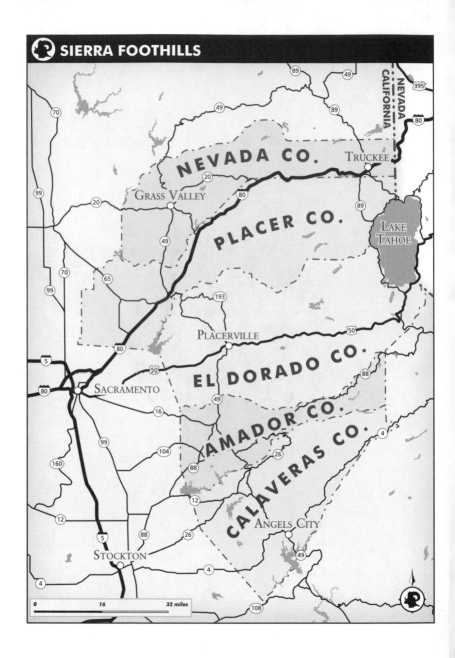

Contents

Introduction · 2

Chapter 1: Nevada County · 15

CHICAGO PARK
1) Montoliva Vineyard and Winery · 18

GRASS VALLEY
2) Lucchesi Vineyards and Winery · 21
3) Sierra Knolls Vineyard and Winery · 24
4) Sierra Starr Vineyard · 26

NEVADA CITY
5) Indian Springs Vineyards · 29
6) Nevada City Winery · 32

PENN VALLEY
7) Pilot Peak Vineyard and Winery · 36

More Area Wineries · 39
Side Trips · 41
For More Information · 44

Chapter 2: Placer County · 47

AUBURN
1) Baumbach Wines · 49
2) Lone Buffalo Vineyards · 53
3) Mt. Vernon Winery · 55
4) Viña Castellano · 58

LOOMIS

5) Secret Ravine Vineyard and Winery — 60

NEWCASTLE

6) Dono dal Cielo Vineyard — 62
7) Ophir Wines — 64

More Area Wineries — 67
Side Trips — 68
For More Information — 70

Chapter 3: El Dorado County — 73

CAMINO

1) Crystal Basin Cellars — 75
2) Findleton Estate and Winery — 78
3) Jodar Vineyards and Winery — 82
4) Madroña Vineyards — 85
5) Wofford Acres Vineyards — 88

FAIR PLAY

6) Colibri Ridge Winery and Vineyard — 91
7) dkcellars — 93
8) Fleur de Lys Winery — 96
9) Granite Springs Winery — 99
10) Iverson Vineyards and Winery — 102
11) Perry Creek Winery — 105
12) Shadow Ranch Vineyard and Winery — 107
13) Sierra Oaks Estates — 110
14) Toogood Estate Winery — 113

MOUNT AUKUM

15) Latcham Vineyards — 115

PLACERVILLE

16) Boeger Winery — 119

17) David Girard Vineyards 124
18) Fenton Herriott Vineyards 128
19) Holly's Hill Vineyards 131
20) Lava Cap Winery 134
21) Narrow Gate Vineyards 138
22) Sierra Vista Vineyards and Winery 141

    SHINGLE SPRINGS
23) Chevalier Winery 145

    SOMERSET
24) Busby Cellars 149
25) Cantiga Wineworks 152
26) Windwalker Vineyard and Winery 156

More Area Wineries 159
Side Trips 164
For More Information 167

Chapter 4: Amador County 169

    IONE
1) Tanis Vineyards 172

    PLYMOUTH
2) Amador Cellars 174
3) Amador Foothill Winery 177
4) Bantam Cellars 180
5) Bray Vineyards 182
6) C. G. Di Arie 185
7) Cooper Vineyards 188
8) Deaver Vineyards 191
9) Dillian Wines 194
10) Dobra Zemlja Winery 195
11) Jeff Runquist Wines 198
12) Karly Wines 200

13) Nine Gables Vineyard and Winery 202
14) Renwood Winery 205
15) Shenandoah Vineyards 209
16) Sobon Estate 212
17) Stonehouse Vineyards and Winery 215
18) Story Winery 217
19) Terra d'Oro Winery 220
20) Terre Rouge and Easton Wines 223
21) TKC Vineyards 226
22) Wilderotter Vineyard and Winery 229

SUTTER CREEK
23) Avio Vineyards 231
24) Sierra Ridge Vineyards and Winery 234

More Area Wineries 237
Side Trips 239
For More Information 241

Chapter 5: Calaveras County 243

DOUGLAS FLAT
1) Chatom Vineyards 246

MOKELUMNE HILL
2) French Hill Winery 248

MURPHYS
3) Beaux Chevaux Tasting Gallery 250
4) Black Sheep Winery 253
5) Bodega del Sur Winery 255
6) Brice Station Vintners 258
7) Domaine Becquet Winery 260
8) Hatcher Winery 264
9) Indian Rock Vineyards 267
10) Ironstone Vineyards 269

11) Milliaire Winery 274
12) Muir's Legacy 277
13) Newsome-Harlow Winery 281
14) Solomon Wine Company 283
15) Tanner Vineyards 286
16) Vina Moda Winery 289
17) Zucca Mountain Vineyards 291

VALLECITO
18) Laraine Winery 294
19) Twisted Oak Winery 297

More Area Wineries 301
Side Trips 303
For More Information 306

Acknowledgments 308

Index 313

About the Authors 320

Introduction

The foothills of the California Sierra Nevada hold many treasures, from gold and lumber to national and state parks to vast recreational opportunities. The region is also known for its history, as gold was discovered here in the foothill community of Coloma in 1848, triggering one of the largest and fastest human migrations the world has ever seen. But today, there's a different kind of gold found in the Sierra foothills, and it is launching another great migration, that of wine lovers and wine enthusiasts.

California's Sierra foothills are home to one of the fastest growing wine regions in the Golden State. Here, hundreds of wineries can be found, many whose roots run deep, all the way back to the 1850s. But the majority of wineries in the foothill region are relatively young, which adds excitement, new technology, and out-of-the-box thinking to the age-old tradition of wine crafting.

The first in a series of *Wine-Oh! Guides,* this book—which focuses on the California Sierra foothills region—shows that there's so much more to wine tasting than purchasing a bottle—there's the tasting adventure, the relaxing and enjoyable ambiance, the chance to spend a wonderful day with family and friends. The great wineries featured in this *Wine-Oh! Guide* are those we would take our friends and family to—and we have—not only for good wine, but also for their history, uniqueness, entertainment, food pairings, and atmosphere.

In doing research for this guide, we visited each and every winery and got to know the owners, and sometimes their kids, staff, and the winemakers (when the winemaker wasn't the owner). We even hung out with established grape growers. From there, we received hands-on training when it came to all aspects of the wine business, from planting to the seasonal harvest and crush to bottling to pouring. And we spent countless hours talking with these folks; a simple question posed by us more times than not turned into wonderful explanations and stories from our new friends. We learned that no one can explain his or her wine in better detail and with as much passion as a devoted wine artisan. Many of those stories are in this guide and more can be found at **www.WineOhGuide.com** (see page 11 for a description of the site). And for the record, we didn't accept bribes to write only good things about the wineries found within, although several owners insisted we take a bottle of their wine to enjoy later!

WINE IN CALIFORNIA

California's wine history began with the Spanish in 1769, when Father Junipero Serra founded his first mission in San Diego. Among his fields of grains, fruits, and beans, he planted grapes to produce wine for religious purposes. It's likely that the Spanish soldiers in this lonely outpost also found uses for the padre's wine. While other varietal grapes were being introduced beginning about 1833, Father Serra's initial vines became known as the "Mission grape," and it dominated California's infant wine industry until the 1880s.

Accompanying California's thirsty Gold Rush 49ers, Hungarian immigrant Agoston Haraszthy began importing cuttings from dozens of different European grape varieties. In 1857, he founded California's first commercial winery in Sonoma and named it Buena Vista Winery (now Buena Vista Carneros). His varietal grapes soon found their way to many parts of California, including the Sierra foothills.

As California's wine industry flourished in the late 19th century, Europe's winemakers were taking a beating as a destructive root louse known as phylloxera was decimating the continent's vineyards. A horticulturalist from Texas, of all places, discovered that phylloxera could be defeated by grafting European vine cuttings onto California grape rootstock, which was largely immune to the deadly pest. While Europe's wine industry was struggling to revive itself, California's wine industry was thriving and its wines were winning gold medals in European wine tastings.

While phylloxera couldn't destroy California's wine industry, the U.S. government could, and did, for decades. The Volstead National Prohibition Act in 1919, and its related Eighteenth Amendment to the Constitution in 1920, prohibited the manufacture, sale, and transport of intoxicating liquors, which included wine. With the market for fine wines wiped out, growers replaced their wine grape vineyards with fruit orchards or inexpensive and low-quality juice grapes. By 1925, wine production in California had dropped by 94 percent. Only a few of the original varietal vines remained where permits allowed for the limited production of wine for medicinal and religious purposes.

Prohibition was repealed in 1933, and California was flooded with cheap, poor-quality wine. Fortified dessert wines became very popular and outsold table wines until the 1960s. Prior to Prohibition there were 2,500 commercial wineries in the U.S. and 781 bonded wineries in California. When Prohibition ended, only 100 wineries remained in the entire nation, and it would take 50 years before California once again reached 781 bonded wineries. Today there are more than 2,800 bonded wineries in the state, with California accounting for 90 percent of the wine produced in the U.S. If California were a country, it would be the fourth-largest producer of wine in the world.

THE SIERRA FOOTHILLS APPELLATION

California is divided into five large wine regions: North Coast, Central Coast, South Coast, Central Valley, and the Sierra Foothills. Within those regions, which are also referred to as "appellations," numerous American

Viticultural Areas (AVAs) exist. Even more confusing, lots of little AVAs can exist inside a larger AVA. For example, the Sierra Foothills AVA contains both the El Dorado AVA and the Fair Play AVA. For most people, AVAs or appellations mean little unless you're a wine drinker. For a wine to advertise on its label that it belongs to a particular AVA (i.e., an El Dorado wine or a Napa Valley wine), 85 percent of the grapes used in that wine must come from the identified AVA.

In the last dozen years or so, the Sierra foothills appellation has matured significantly as a producer of fine wines. With a foothill climate similar to that of wine-producing areas in France, Bordeaux-style wines have become very popular in the region. Red wines such as Cabernet Sauvignon, Cabernet Franc, and Merlot grow well in both France and the Sierra foothills. This popularity also applies to the Rhone varieties found in southern France that include Syrah and Viognier. Italian red varietals, including Sangiovese and Barbera, along with white Pinot Grigio, are popular in the Sierra foothills. One of the most popular and oldest wines here is Zinfandel, a red grape that is apparently distantly related to Primitivo (Italy) and Crljenak Kastelanski (Croatia). While the red version of California's Zinfandel is prized for its robust and fruity taste, the white version—White Zinfandel—sells about six times as much in volume each year. Many more varietals than these are grown in the Sierra foothills with varying levels of success.

Most Sierra foothill wineries, especially the smaller boutique wineries, specialize in one or two varietals and perhaps a few blends. Some wineries grow their own grapes, while many more depend on grapes purchased from local or regional grape growers who are not necessarily winemakers. A few wineries also use grapes from outside their appellation.

In the U.S., most wines identified on their labels as a varietal—Cabernet Sauvignon, Merlot, Zinfandel, and so forth—must contain at least 75 percent of the named grape. Concord grape–based wines, which are rare in the Sierra foothills, require less, only 51 percent. Most winemakers create excellent blends by taking two or more varietal grapes and combining them into a single wine with new and different taste characteristics. These wines are the ones that end up with nonvarietal grape names on their bottles such as Mother Lode Red or Crestview Gold.

USING THIS BOOK

Wine-Oh! Guides are designed to be easy to use, comprehensive, and fun. The series introduces wine lovers to many of the lesser-known wine regions, with stories about those unique and eclectic wineries and their just-as-interesting wine owners, winemakers, and grape growers. The California Sierra foothills guide is divided into five chapters, one for each county from north to south: Nevada, Placer, El Dorado, Amador, and Calaveras counties. Each chapter begins with an introduction that provides a short history of each county, much of it Gold Rush history. Each chapter's locator map corresponds with that chapter's wineries. From there, you're free to peruse the many winery listings, discovering the richness of each destination and its contribution to the wine industry. And if you want to learn more about a particular winery, each listing has contact information, including a website. Additional wineries not covered in detail are included in "More Area Wineries" sections after the main listings.

Since there is much to see and do in the Sierra foothills in addition to visiting the wineries, we have suggested side trips to museums, historic parks, and more. Each chapter also provides a contact list for local and regional visitor bureaus, wine organizations, and such.

SELECTION CRITERIA

While using this guide, you'll find that wineries weren't selected based on their size or how many gold medals their wines have won. The wineries featured herein range from mom-and-pop operations that produce as few as 50 cases a year to those household names that produce 500,000 cases a year!

Those wineries featured by way of a full story qualified for such because: 1) They each completed our consideration survey as required, providing enough information to help us create a usable story, 2) They have regularly posted public hours, and 3) When we visited each candidate winery, we determined their business was worthy of being included. For those wineries listed without a story, it was either that they responded but did not complete the survey in full or in detail, or that they were a reputable winery in that particular region and their inclusion was warranted. If we have inadvertently missed a winery or two, we offer apologies in advance. But considering we visited more than 150 wineries while doing our research, we did our best. And we must thank all of our friends who offered to go along with us as "research buddies"—if we had actually tasted all the wines graciously offered at each winery, this book would still be in its first draft!

While we're on the topic of tasting, the reason we didn't "partake" at most of the wineries was that we are not—in any way, shape, or form—wine critics. We're simply wine lovers. It wouldn't be fair for us to formally evaluate any winery's bottled offerings because, quite honestly, almost all offer great wines and choosing the "best" wine from among the hundreds of tastings offered is subjective.

While some consider the stereotypical "Two-Buck Chuck" (Charles Shaw) to be a good wine buy, others prefer more complex wines that typically exceed $2 a bottle. For this reason, we usually don't go much beyond mentioning those varietals and blends that a winery is known for and leaving it at that. As the old saying goes, "To each his own." Everyone's tastes and taste buds are different, which means nobody is ever 100 percent right about what is a great wine, good wine, or bad wine. How do you choose a great bottle of wine from among the thousands of choices out there? It's easy—buy what you like.

With this guide in hand, it's time for you to head to California's Sierra foothills. Taste, experience, and enjoy—and take a few bottles home to share with family and friends. They will love you for it.

BEFORE YOU GO

Before you go, be sure to contact the winery or destination as hours of operation can change without notice. Their contact information appears at the end of each listing.

Also, if you will be visiting via a tour bus or limousine service, it is strongly encouraged that you notify the winery prior to your visit. While many will welcome you with open arms, others require advance notification or they will not serve you and your party, or they may charge an additional fee to taste.

And last, the majority of wineries in this book offer complimentary tastings, which harkens back to the days of Napa and Sonoma counties when the living was easy and the wine tastings were free. And we all know what happened there, as today $5 a taste isn't unheard of in either county.

As true wine lovers know—and winemakers and winery owners will concede—operating a winery is a business, and that business needs sales to keep offering complimentary tastings. Quite simply, if you love a wine, please buy a bottle or two or even an entire case, and show your support for these wonderful Sierra foothill wineries.

WEBSITE BONUS

During our travels, we learned so much that we couldn't fit it all into this book. On our website **www.WineOh Guide.com,** you'll find in-depth interviews with numerous winemakers, grape growers, and winery owners. They're passionate about their craft and their wine; you'll learn what makes them tick and why they love the business. Plus, you'll enjoy their unique sense of humor. And boy, do they have intriguing stories to share. We'll be adding more interviews—so visit often.

We can't forget the food! Winemakers will tell you to drink the wine you like and eat the foods you love. There are no set rules for what wines go with which foods; so much for the myth that red wines go only with red meat or white wines with white meat. Pairing your favorite port with rich, chocolate brownies will likely add to the pleasure of both, as might combining crab cakes with your Chardonnay, Viognier, or even a Merlot. Several wineries offer pairing opportunities, especially at their wine club member dinners. If you would like to experience some great food and wine pairings, go to our website **www.WineOhGuide. com.** We are constantly adding new food and wine pairing ideas, along with delicious recipes from our favorite wineries.

Besides the interviews and food, the website includes more fun photographs, a wine blog with guest contributors, and links to winery websites. You can also become an official "Wine-Oh!" by signing up for our quarterly e-newsletter that includes book and winery updates, featured articles, winery discount coupons, plus announcements regarding new *Wine-Oh! Guides.*

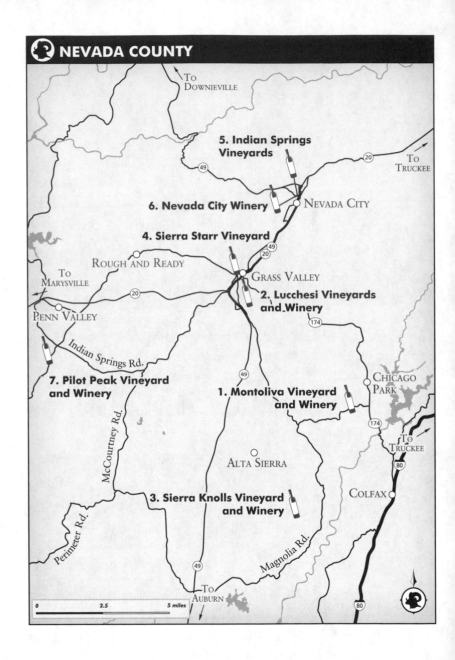

NEVADA COUNTY

To DOWNIEVILLE

5. Indian Springs Vineyards

To TRUCKEE

6. Nevada City Winery

NEVADA CITY

4. Sierra Starr Vineyard

ROUGH AND READY

To MARYSVILLE

GRASS VALLEY

2. Lucchesi Vineyards and Winery

PENN VALLEY

Indian Springs Rd.

7. Pilot Peak Vineyard and Winery

CHICAGO PARK

1. Montoliva Vineyard and Winery

To TRUCKEE

ALTA SIERRA

COLFAX

3. Sierra Knolls Vineyard and Winery

McCourtney Rd.

Perimeter Rd.

Magnolia Rd.

To AUBURN

0   2.5   5 miles

★ Nevada County

Nevada County is rich in Gold Rush history. The 49ers first panned the loose, easily accessible placer gold from rivers and streams. In 1850, George Roberts discovered gold locked in quartz rock where today's Empire Mine State Historic Park is located. His discovery created a hard-rock mining frenzy as hundreds of miners flooded the area, staking their 30- by 40-foot claims where they dug 20- to 40-foot-deep "coyote holes" searching for gold-bearing quartz.

The miners quickly discovered that extracting gold from rock was both laborious and dangerous. Most miners soon sold their claims to big companies that could afford the expense of digging miles of deep tunnels and obtaining the huge stamp mills required to crush tons of ore in order to extract the gold. The North Star, Empire, and Idaho-Maryland mines took millions of dollars' worth of gold from deep underground mines, making Grass Valley and Nevada City

California's center for hard-rock mining. The Empire Mine alone extracted 5.6 million ounces of gold from its 367 miles of tunnels before it closed in 1956.

Millions of dollars of placer, or loose, gold lay buried in nearby hillsides. In 1853, innovative miners began hydraulic mining operations to uncover the treasure. Using large "guns" called monitors, they directed powerful streams of water at hillsides, ultimately washing away entire mountains. The slurry of eroded gravels was then processed for the gold it contained. Hydraulic mining was outlawed in 1884, but the resulting landscape devastation can still be seen today at Malakoff Diggins State Historic Park, located north of Nevada City.

While the miners were mining, the cities around them were growing. Nevada County was created in 1851 from land that was originally part of Yuba County and was named after the bustling mining town of Nevada City. Even though the mines are closed, there remains plenty to do here, especially when it comes to wine tasting in the region's many wineries. Both Grass Valley and Nevada City have historic downtowns with dozens of gift and antique shops and many fine restaurants—some simple and inexpensive, others serving fancier fare.

For those wineries outside of town, two-lane country roads offer spectacular views throughout this rural landscape. From horses and cattle quietly grazing to hawks hunting their next meal, there is plenty to explore and enjoy away from the bustle of even small-town life.

CHICAGO PARK

1 Montoliva Vineyard and Winery

Even though Montoliva Vineyard and Winery's mailing address is Grass Valley, the business is 10 miles southeast in the quaint community of Chicago Park. "Chicago Park was originally settled and named by first-generation Italian-Americans who moved here from Chicago. We are continuing the tradition they started," explained owner and winemaker Mark Henry. Henry and his wife Julianne opened their business in 2000. Producing upward of 1,500 cases a year, the winery's name translates in Italian to "Mount Olive," the name of the road on which the winery is found.

Henry started out as a beermaker and owned a small chain of amateur beer and winemaking stores in Seattle in the 1990s. The business did so well that Henry began an import business, in part supplying Canadian winemakers with grape concentrate from Australia. Realizing that actually knowing how to make wine would help his import business, Henry taught himself the art form. He fell in love with winemaking and ended up in Italy, receiving hands-on training about old-world techniques in Montalcino, Tuscany. He now produces Tuscan-inspired luxury wines, at, what Henry notes, are "value prices."

Montoliva's award-winning Sangiovese

This self-proclaimed farmer and lover of wine is quite the character (to learn more about Henry, read his interview at **www.WineOhGuide.com**) and absolutely loves what he does. "I started out as a beermaker. That got boring," Henry said. "Winemaking is a lot of things. Boring isn't one of them."

WINE MYTH } **One person's myth is another person's oral history.**
—Mark Henry

Henry has a point. Bucking the trend in the Golden State to make what he calls "the fruit-forward, new-world style of winemaking that is dominant in California," Henry feels that Italian varietals such as Sangiovese are better served by employing the old-world style he learned in Italy. His goal is to make "lean, powerful wines that display a more subtle front-end, an earthy mid-palate, and a lingering finish." This holds true when it comes to Montoliva's signature Sangiovese; Henry is carrying on the pioneering spirit of Chicago Park's Italian settlers.

The winery's small tasting room is at the back of the property, facing the sloping vineyard. Pointing out at his field, Henry said, "The original Donner Trail passes through the vineyard. However, we don't encourage cannibalism."

What the couple does encourage, or rather embrace wholeheartedly, is sustainable agriculture. Their vineyards are pesticide free, they use a highly-regulated drip irrigation system, and they compost all of their press-ings. The Henrys invite visitors to meander through their extensive herb garden, which varies from basil to tarragon to chives. And yes, they encourage picking.

FEATURED WINE: Sangiovese
TASTING COST: Complimentary
HOURS: Saturday and Sunday, 12 PM–5 PM
LOCATION: 15629 Mount Olive Road, Grass Valley
PHONE: 530-346-6577
WEBSITE: www.montoliva.com

GRASS VALLEY

2 *Lucchesi Vineyards and Winery*

Lucchesi Vineyards and Winery opened in 2002. Owner Mario Clough noted that his "View Forever Vineyard," with its 20 steeply terraced acres, is unique for the area: "Great care was taken in selecting the grape varieties and clones that are best suited to the soil. The southwestern exposure maximizes the sun's rays, perfectly ripening the fruit with concentrated flavor, color, and texture. As a result, some of the finest grapes in the Sierra foothills grow in our vineyards and are the origin of our finely crafted wines."

Lucchesi is steeped in family history. When asked about the origins of the vineyard's name, Clough

Lucchesi's quaint tasting room in Grass Valley

shared, "The Lucchesi family origins lie in Provincia Di Lucca, Toscana, and we are the direct descendants from the civilization of the Etruscans, the native culture of northwestern/central Italy, and first civilization of Italy and the Romans." Mario's family left Italy for Egypt in the late 1930s to escape the oppression of Benito Mussolini. As Nazi forces invaded North Africa, his family moved again to South America. After his father died, his mother married Forest Lynn Clough, an American, who adopted Mario and his sister, and the Clough family moved to the U.S.

Besides the tasting room at the winery proper, Lucchesi Vineyards and Winery has a trendy tasting room in downtown Grass Valley on the corner of Mill and Neal streets, under the large and stately steeple for the historic Del Oro Theatre—you can't miss it. Inside, the tasting room is stylish and well-designed for its small size, and friendly staff members are eager to pour tastings and answer questions. You'll also find gourmet food and gift baskets for sale, as well as the vineyard's logo items and elegant wines.

FEATURED WINES: Chardonnay, Cabernet Franc, Cabernet Sauvignon, and Zinfandel
TASTING COST: Complimentary
PHONE: 888-923-4423 or 530-273-1596
WEBSITE: www.lucchesivineyards.com

WINERY
HOURS: Friday and Saturday, 11:30 AM–6 PM; Sunday–Thursday, 11:30 AM–5 PM (call ahead as they sometimes are closed for special events)
LOCATION: 19698 View Forever Lane, Grass Valley

TASTING ROOM
HOURS: Daily, 11 AM–5 PM
LOCATION: 167 Mill Street, Grass Valley

3 *Sierra Knolls Vineyard and Winery*

A visit to Sierra Knolls Vineyard and Winery is like a treasure hunt. Located in southern Grass Valley about 7 miles off of Highway 49, the winery's street address can be confusing. Despite their mailing address of Kingswood "Court," they are on a road instead, and it's a mile's drive up a long hill to get there. Signage is hard to see and don't rely on your GPS; visit the winery's website for a detailed map and directions before you go.

With that said, once you get to Sierra Knolls, you will have found treasure galore! At an elevation of 2300 feet, the view alone is worth the trek; on clear days, you can see the Sacramento Valley and coastal range, and sunset is a real treat. Their landscaped grounds are gorgeous, and picnics are strongly encouraged. You'll also discover a 50-foot-deep, hand-dug wine barrel cave and their charming tasting room, where the friendly staff will go the extra mile to make sure your visit is enjoyable.

This small family-owned operation opened in 2000 and is owned by John and Linda Chase and Steve and Brenda Taylor, all close friends for many years. Linda explained, "We started making wine as home winemakers and our wines began to win awards. We planted [our] vineyard on 45 acres and opened the winery. It's a hobby gone crazy!"

Linda's husband John, an engineer who enjoys the chemistry aspect of making wine, oversees the process.

The wine cave at Sierra Knolls

"We depend on our family and friends to help us with harvest, bottling, and staffing our events. [Our] son Scott helps with the winemaking duties and daughter Sara makes a wine we call 'Saravese,'" Linda added. One interesting aside is that the winery and grounds run completely on solar energy.

Since it's a touch out of the way, call before visiting to make sure the tasting room is open, even during posted hours (their website states they may be closed some weekends).

FEATURED WINES: Barbera and Sangiovese
TASTING COST: Complimentary
HOURS: Saturday and Sunday, 11 AM–5 PM (call ahead to confirm)
LOCATION: 19635 Kingswood Court, Grass Valley
PHONE: 530-268-9225
WEBSITE: www.sierraknollswinery.com

4 *Sierra Starr Vineyard*

Sierra Starr Vineyard's tasting room, on West Main Street in historic downtown Grass Valley, is where you'll find "Fine Wine, Fun People . . . Starr Quality!" Anne and Phil Starr launched their business in 1995. Prior to moving to the foothills, they owned Elkhorn Farms in Monterey County, providing specialty-cut flowers to the florist trade for more than two decades.

A farmer at heart, Phil Starr's foray into winemaking is a fun story, especially since he obtained his degree—two in fact—from Chico State University, known as the "party school" (to learn more, read Starr's interview at **www.WineOhGuide.com**). Now son Jackson is vineyard manager and assistant winemaker. "It's a privilege and rare opportunity to be able to work with and mentor one's child. We consider ourselves very fortunate to have our son Jackson working with us each day. The added fact that our passion has become his [passion] is 'icing on the cake,'" beamed a proud dad.

When asked what makes their wine special, Starr said that besides using wild yeast fermentation on several of their wines, they use traditional methods of cold stabilization during the seasonably cold winter. "This means

WINE MYTH } *"Legs" on the sides of a wine glass after swirling means that the wine is of a better quality. It means nothing as to the quality of the wine.* —**Phil Starr**

Wilfred Wietstock

Sierra Starr's tasting room is the place to be!

we put the wine outside in January and February," Starr laughed.

Sierra Starr's wares are estate-made at their combination vineyard and winery proper in Grass Valley, which is open only for special events such as their summer picnic and concert event series "Music in the Vineyard" or arranged group tours. Their tasting room, found at the clock tower in Grass Valley's historic district, is open daily. The Starr family has done a remarkable job restoring the building, which was built in 1870. A restored rock wall, made of mine rock quarried from local gold mines more than 140 years ago, complements the original red brick on the opposite wall, painstakingly brought back to life by hand. The west half of the floor was revealed after removing carpet, linoleum, and finally black-glued, gunnysack-backed tile. Modern touches include a gentle S-curved bar, custom made by Starr, and a gorgeous hand-painted mural depicting their nearby vineyard/winery. Local artist Rainn painted it and hand-carved the tasting room's breathtaking front door.

The Starr's official greeter is their bloodhound mix Chewy, who happily inspects customers at the door. "He's a pound dog, and when we first saw him, he looked fierce," said Starr. While Chewy loves the attention—and the treats and holiday presents he receives from regulars—he's also protective and has been known to sniff and lick guests of all ages like crazy.

Having a last name like "Starr" lends itself nicely to the winery's use of celestial wine labels. For instance, there's Solstice Sauvignon Blanc, Milky Way Merlot, and Starr Dust Cabernet Sauvignon, to name a few. One fanciful and popular wine is their ice wine—Celestial Delight—which is perfect for those hot summer days. And one of their more popular wines, Zinjolais, comes out right before Thanksgiving; its creation process is unique to the Beaujolais region of France. To learn more about this famous wine making process, read Starr's interview at **www.WineOhGuide.com.**

Another celestial name is their Sirius Sipper Wine Club. Anne Starr noted that they named the club for an especially important heavenly body: "Sirius is the brightest star in the sky, just in case you thought it was only a radio station."

FEATURED WINES: Sauvignon Blanc and Zinfandel
TASTING COST: Complimentary, with the exception of port
or ice wine—$2 (applied toward purchase)
HOURS: Daily, 12 PM–5 PM
LOCATION: 124 West Main Street, Grass Valley
PHONE: 530-477-8282
WEBSITE: www.sierrastarr.com

NEVADA CITY

5 *Indian Springs Vineyards*

The charm of historic Nevada City draws tourists from
all over the world. From antique hunting to great meals
to window shopping, the town offers myriad opportunities to experience the wealth of this small Mother
Lode community.

One such find is the tasting room for Indian Springs
Vineyards. Located on Broad Street—the main drag—
it's a favorite stop as is evident from their continuously
busy tasting bar. Here they offer a huge list of wines
under many different labels, including a U2 wine. Per
Indian Springs's website, this label is dedicated to the
famed spy plane. They also have fanciful labels that include such fun offerings as Hog Wild Red Table Wine.
The tasting notes about the wine state, "This wine is a
real ham."

Indian Springs's tasting room entrance

Indian Springs was founded by Dennis Ball in the early 1980s. His vineyard is in Penn Valley—on Indian Springs Road—and isn't open to the public, and his wines are bottled in Lake County's Kelseyville under the watchful eye of winemaker Jed Steele of Steele Vineyards. A veteran of the wine industry for more than 40 years, Steele started both Edmeandes Winery in Anderson Valley and Kendall-Jackson, leaving the year they broke the 1 million cases per year production mark. In 1991, he established his self-named winery—Steele Vineyards (www.steelewines.com).

The tasting room is a treat in and of itself, especially if you like shopping. While enjoying your wine, you can peruse the many gift items, including high-end kitchen and winery merchandise.

FEATURED WINES: Syrah, Cabernet Franc, and Barbera
TASTING COST: Complimentary
HOURS: Friday and Saturday, 11:30 AM–6 PM; Sunday–Thursday, 11:30 AM–5 PM
LOCATION: 303 Broad Street, Nevada City
PHONE: 800-375-9311 or 530-478-1068
WEBSITE: www.indianspringswines.com

6 *Nevada City Winery*

Nevada City's oldest winery is aptly named Nevada City Winery. On Spring Street, just one block south of the town's main drag, you'll experience some of the finest wines in the county. The winery had auspicious beginnings; established in 1980 in a small garage just outside of town, business boomed and two years later the need for more room became apparent. The winery moved into a bigger building in town—the historic Miners Foundry Garage.

"We are the first modern winery in Nevada County," explained winemaker Mark Foster, noting that their current location was originally built in the 1880s as a carriage house for the Miners Foundry next door. "And remarkably we stand two blocks from the original Nevada City Winery, which produced 5,000 cases of wines in 1885 from local grapes," he continued, citing that the original winery was on Spring Street behind the still-standing historic National Hotel.

Today's Nevada City Winery has played a strong philanthropic role in keeping the town's major historic building a part of the community. The Miners Foundry Complex, which opened in 1856 and supplied the region with industrial metalworking, closed in the 1960s. It became a museum and restaurant, but the owner eventually filed for bankruptcy.

WINE MYTH } **White wines don't age very well.** **Some of our Gewürztraminers are more than 20 years old and when we open a bottle, there is a battle over who gets to take the rest of the bottle home. They get so unctuous and complex with age.**

—Mark Foster

When a developer was considering buying the building to open a shopping mall, Nevada City Winery stepped in and purchased it for a substantial amount of money. It was at that point a nonprofit was formed, and the winery sold the building to the nonprofit for one dollar. Today, the complex is home to a museum and very active community center. "We just had to do it," said Foster, noting that while the winery took a huge financial loss on the deal, helping their community, one that has embraced them for more than 30 years, was the right thing to do.

The first bonded winery to open in Nevada County following Prohibition, Nevada City Winery makes their wines on the premises, below the tasting room. Guided tours are offered on Saturdays at 1:30 PM; if your group is larger than 10 people, it's best to call ahead. And if you're lucky, it will be Foster, with more than 15 years of experience at the winery, leading the tour; you'll quickly realize that he truly loves what he does (to learn more about Foster, read his interview at **www.WineOhGuide.com**).

In the tasting room, an attractive gift shop features high-end gourmet products, glassware, jewelry, and other

Entrance to Nevada City Winery

unique items. And when you mosey over to the tasting bar, be sure to look down at the bar itself: It's a restored bowling alley from the Nevada City Elks Club. The wood is old-growth yellow pine and is said to be more than 120 years old. The single-lane bowling alley was on the second floor of a downtown building until 1930 when the downstairs tenants complained, thus bringing a halt to the noisy game. Nearly 50 years later, the bowling alley was taken out as one piece and thrown onto a garbage pile. Foster saw the wood and asked if the winery could take it. The answer was a resounding "yes," and the historic item is now enjoying a second life as a winery tasting room bar.

Nevada City Winery is a wonderful first stop on your visit to this historic Gold Rush town. Their tasting room staff is extremely friendly and knowledgeable and double as terrific tour guides: They can tell you about great places to eat or shops to visit in the city and surrounding area. And if you happen to meet their wine dog Spencer, you'll be showered with affection. He was recently featured in the popular, nationwide Wine Dogs series (www.winedogs.com).

FEATURED WINES: Cabernet Franc, Syrah, Zinfandel, and Petit Verdot
TASTING COST: Complimentary
HOURS: Friday and Saturday, 12 PM–6 PM; Sunday–Thursday, 12 PM–6 PM
LOCATION: 321 Spring Street, Nevada City
PHONE: 800-203-9463 or 530-265-9463
WEBSITE: www.ncwinery.com

PENN VALLEY

7 *Pilot Peak Vineyard and Winery*

 Pilot Peak Vineyard and Winery, in Penn Valley off of Highway 20, is the only winery in the Sierra foothills to offer a comparative tasting experience. For those not familiar with comparative tasting, it's just what it sounds like: You compare wines while tasting. You're probably saying to yourself, "Isn't that what I do anyway whenever I taste?" Yes, but winery owners Jacque and Lynn Wilson do it with style.

When you arrive, the Pilot Peak team greets you and pours you a glass of white wine. They then ask you what kind of wine you like, and while you help yourself to a small buffet (with at least three different appetizers) they prepare a flight of four wines for your tasting. Once you are seated on their large stone-walled terrace (weather permitting), they will bring you your flight. Each glass is numbered and you're given a corresponding tasting sheet. It's as easy as that, and believe it or not, it's free! Pilot Peak's brochure boldly states, "Come try this new tasting method and you'll never want to go back to the old way of tasting wines." They might just be right!

Wine is served in "flight" glasses.

Jacque retired after 30 years in the technical information systems and financial management fields for some of the world's biggest companies. She shared that her husband Lynn, who is the winemaker, is also "an excellent chef, wonderful husband, and friend!" A retired aeronautical engineer, Lynn learned the craft of winemaking through courses at the University of California at Davis. "It's hard to believe that we started all of this from scratch," Lynn said, and he wasn't talking about his latest recipe, but about the winery, which opened in 2004.

And it's quite the place. The drive alone is a treat as you meander through hill and dale, even through a working ranch with horses, barns, and farm equipment on both sides. When you arrive at the winery's entrance, you'll think you're visiting an estate as you pass through a wrought-iron gate and head uphill on a concrete driveway (something not commonly seen in the country). At the top, you'll find the Wilsons' stunning Mediterranean-style winery, nestled beneath a stand of oaks. Inside the California "rustic-chic" tasting room are two tasting bars. Again, weather permitting, most guests will be on the oversized terrace soaking in the fine wine, gourmet food, and great views, including that of nearby Pilot Peak.

The Wilsons offer two labels: their standard Pilot Peak wines (medium- to full-bodied) and the whimsically labeled "PeaK A Boo" series (light- to medium-bodied). Talking with the Wilsons, it's obvious that Jacque is a marketing pro; one wine—PeaK A Boo LiVedo—has a fun translation. *LiVedo* means "I see you" in Italian.

FEATURED WINES: Viognier and Syrah
TASTING COST: Complimentary
HOURS: Saturday and Sunday, 12 PM–5 PM
LOCATION: 12888 Spenceville Road, Penn Valley
PHONE: 530-432-3321
WEBSITE: www.pilotpeak.com

✛ More Area Wineries

GRASS VALLEY

Avanguardia Wines
HOURS: Daily, 12 PM–5 PM
LOCATION: 209 West Main Street, Grass Valley
PHONE: 530-274-9911
WEBSITE: www.avanguardiawines.com

Naggiar Vineyards and Winery
HOURS: Friday–Sunday, 12 PM–5 PM
LOCATION: 18125 Rosemary Lane, Grass Valley
PHONE: 530-268-9059
WEBSITE: www.naggiarvineyards.com

Solune Winery
HOURS: Saturday and Sunday, 12 PM–5 PM
LOCATION: 16303 Jewett Lane, Grass Valley
PHONE: 530-271-0990
WEBSITE: www.solunewinery.com

NEVADA CITY

Double Oak Vineyards and Winery
HOURS: February–December, Saturday, 11 AM–5 PM
LOCATION: 14510 Blind Shady Road, Nevada City
PHONE: 530-292-3235
WEBSITE: www.doubleoakwinery.com

ROUGH AND READY

Coufos Cellars
HOURS: Saturday, 12 PM–5 PM
LOCATION: 10065 Rough and Ready Road, Rough and Ready
PHONE: 530-274-2923
WEBSITE: None listed

SIDE TRIPS

California's gold country history goes back thousands of years—millions if you include the geologic formations that created the great pockets of gold that still lace the Sierra foothills. Nevada County is part of an area that was commonly referred to as the "Northern Mines." While homes, businesses, and vineyards grace many of the hillsides today, there's still a lot of opportunities to find your own gold, be it in an antique store—and there are plenty to choose from—or in one of the many historic parks, museums, mines, and towns.

In kind of a miniature grand canyon created by the hand of man—and the use of giant squirt guns called monitors—**Malakoff Diggins State Historic Park** (www.parks.ca.gov) illustrates the destructive side of gold-mining operations in the late 1800s. While washing away mountainsides with powerful streams of water was an efficient gold-mining technique, it also washed millions of cubic yards of mountainsides down rivers, causing floods and even filling in part of San Francisco Bay.

Getting to Malakoff is half the fun—north of Nevada City, you head farther north on North Bloomfield Road, a narrow, steep, and twisting road that leads down to a bridge across the Yuba River. From there you travel along a dirt road out to the mostly abandoned mining town of **North**

Bloomfield, which is now part of the state historic park. Drinking wine before the drive isn't suggested, but you may want a few glasses after you arrive.

There is an alternative route that lets you stay on paved roads—drive 11 miles north from Nevada City on Highway 49, turn right on Tyler Foote Road and follow it to the park. The road changes names several times along the way (Cruzon Grade Road, Back Bone Road, Derbeck Road, and finally North Bloomfield Road). It takes about 50 minutes to drive the 26 miles, but it's a great place for a picnic and short hikes, including one through a historic tunnel that served as a giant drain for the mining operations. The site has a museum and a few historic buildings where you may even see a blacksmith or two working. There's also a pond where kids can fish and a creek where you can do a little gold panning yourself.

For the slightly less adventurous, **Nevada City** (www.nevadacitychamber.com) is home to historic Gold Rush–era buildings that today are restaurants, antique shops, and more. One of the most photographed cities in the Sierra foothills, the town is steeped in history. The **Miners Foundry Cultural Center** (www.minersfoundry.org/index. cfm) is one of those historic buildings, where beginning in 1855, it fabricated the heavy machines and equipment needed to mine gold on a large scale. Also found in Nevada City is the **Nevada County Narrow Gauge Railroad Museum** (www.ncngrrmuseum.org) dedicated to the preservation of local transportation history and artifacts from the narrow gauge railroad era.

Driving south on Highway 49, you'll find the county's biggest city—**Grass Valley**. If you love to go antiquing and boutique shopping, look no farther than **Downtown Grass Valley** (www.downtowngrassvalley.com). The historic district is chock-full of every kind of shop imaginable. On the corner of Mill Street and McCourtney Road, you'll find the **North Star Power House and Pelton Wheel Mining Exhibit** (530-273-4255), which houses mining equipment from the 1880s. On display is the largest Pelton Wheel ever constructed and used to generate power for mining operations, as well as the largest operational Cornish pump. The museum also has a secluded picnic area alongside Wolf Creek.

Just a few miles east of Grass Valley is **Empire Mine State Historic Park** (www.parks.ca.gov). This is one of California's deepest, oldest, largest, and richest hard-rock gold mines, having produced 5.6 million ounces of gold during its 100 years of operation. Today the park includes not only the owner's home that is open for tours, but a mine shaft and the support buildings and equipment used to crush gold ore and separate it from the quartz, then melt and pour the gold into ingots for shipment to San Francisco.

SIDE TRIPS

For More Information

Northern Sierra Wine Country
P.O. Box 1552
Grass Valley, CA 95945
866-355-WINE (9463)
www.nswinecountry.com

Grass Valley/Nevada County Chamber of Commerce
248 Mill Street
Grass Valley, CA 95945
800-655-4667 or 530-273-4667
www.grassvalleychamber.com

Nevada City Chamber of Commerce
132 Main Street
Nevada City, CA 95959
800-655-NJOY or 530-265-2692
www.nevadacitychamber.com

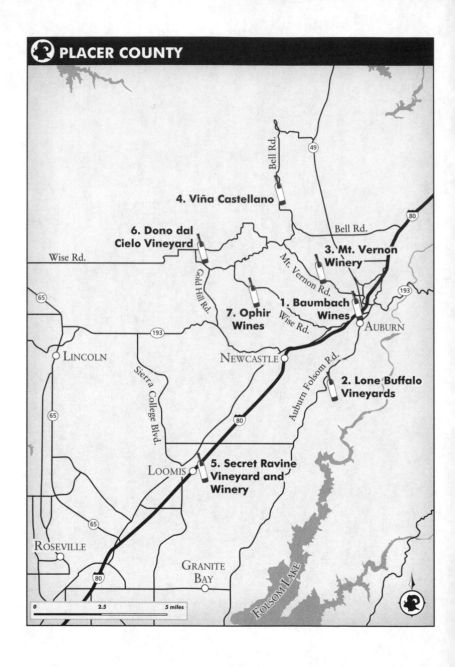

PLACER COUNTY

4. Viña Castellano

6. Dono dal Cielo Vineyard

Wise Rd.

Bell Rd.

Bell Rd.

3. Mt. Vernon Winery

Mt. Vernon Rd.

1. Baumbach Wines

AUBURN

7. Ophir Wines

Wise Rd.

Gold Hill Rd.

LINCOLN

NEWCASTLE

2. Lone Buffalo Vineyards

Sierra College Blvd.

Auburn Folsom Rd.

LOOMIS

5. Secret Ravine Vineyard and Winery

ROSEVILLE

GRANITE BAY

FOLSOM LAKE

0   2.5   5 miles

the Sierra Foothills

2

★ Placer County

P lacer County is a mixture of elevations and opportunities. One of their tourism slogans used to
be "From sea level to ski level" due to the drastic
elevation change; the far western boundary begins in
the Central Valley then stretches east to Lake Tahoe
and the Nevada state line. Continue traveling east on
Interstate 80, which meanders back and forth between
Placer and Nevada counties on its way to Donner Summit, and you pass through an outdoor paradise. Some
of the county's Sierra peaks reach over 9000 feet, making it the perfect place for ski resorts—and there are
plenty to choose from, including Squaw Valley, home
of the 1960 Winter Olympics.

Along the western slope of the Sierra foothills, an
area dubbed the "Northern Mines" by the 49ers, French
immigrant Claude Chana discovered his own golden
opportunity when he planted the first wine grapes—
traditional Mission grapes—in Placer County in 1848.
Italian winemaker and immigrant Stephen Burdge

widened those initial footsteps into history in 1854 when he produced the first commercial wines in the county. Within a year, Zinfandel grapes made their appearance on the rocky hillsides, followed by more growers in the late 1850s planting additional European varietals. By the mid-1860s, Placer County's wine industry was one of the largest in the state.

Travel the roads of Placer County and you'll come across many wineries. Like most of the Sierra foothills, the area experiences very warm summer days and cool evenings as breezes come down off the mountains. Because the majority of the county's wineries are found between 800 and 2000 feet in elevation, the perfect climate combines with near perfect soils to create great viticultural opportunities—something that Claude Chana discovered more than 150 years ago.

AUBURN

1 *Baumbach Wines*

A small Auburn winery, founded by Benjamin Bernhard, has been serving the public since 1874. Current proprietor Neal Baumbach has been carrying on the tradition of handmade fine estate wines since, in 1999, he opened Baumbach Wines in the original building.

"My winery building is one of the oldest winery buildings in active use today," said Baumbach, also a local area physician. On a plaque above the winery's entrance, it reads, in part: "Old Rock Vineyard built in 1874 by Benjamin Bernhard. Rich Flat nearby was one of Auburn's richest gold areas." Built into the hillside, Bernhard's original winery stone walls tower more than two stories high and barrels of wine line the interior walls. According to Baumbach, the structure was built with the help of Chinese laborers and was a favorite spot for miners and travelers. If only the walls could talk, imagine what tales and yarns they would share!

Baumbach Wines produces about 500 cases a year. When asked about his interest in the craft, Baumbach replied, "I enjoyed red wines and wished to make a superior Italian palette of wines." True to his word, the

WINE MYTH } **My favorite myth is actually a misconception by many people that other fruits are added to the wine to give it the fruity flavors. I explain that grapes themselves carry the flavors and this reflects the natural law of conservation by Mother Nature. In other words, the chemical aromatics in grapes and hence wine, are shared by other fruits/aromatics, e.g., apricots, plums, vanilla, pepper, leather, tobacco, etc. —Neal Baumbach**

winery produces limited amounts of Italian varietals such as Charbono, Aglianico, and Nebbiolo, three varietals not commonly found in the Sierra foothills. He explains, "I perform all the steps of wine production from growing several of the varietals to sales. I love the freedom and personal rewards of creating wines with my own creative initiatives. I particularly enjoy the combined scientific and artistic challenge of converting grapes into wine, which others will purchase and enjoy."

Directly behind Baumbach Wines is the former home of Benjamin Bernhard, now part of the city's Bernhard Museum Complex. The home, built in 1851, was originally a hotel for area miners, as well as teamsters traveling Auburn Folsom Road (if you look closely, you'll see that the old road runs directly in front of the museum). The building passed through several

**Historic Baumbach Winery (foreground)
and Bernhard Museum to the right**

owners, then in 1868, the Bernhard family purchased it, occupying the home for the next century. The white Victorian-style home, which is one of Auburn's oldest surviving buildings, has been turned into a museum, and period-dressed docents lead tours. The museum offers free admission and is open 11 AM–4 PM Tuesday–Sunday.

Regarding parking, try the Bernhard Museum parking lot on Maple Street (road leading into the Placer County Fairgrounds). If the museum is closed, leave a note on your dashboard that you're at the winery—the signs state MUSEUM PARKING ONLY, but Baumbach says he's working on getting them changed to include the winery. Since the entrance to the winery is on Auburn Folsom, simply head down the small hill to the sidewalk, take a right and you'll practically be there!

FEATURED WINES: Charbono, Barbera, Zinfandel, and Aglianico
TASTING COST: $5 per person, applied toward purchase
HOURS: Saturday and Sunday, 12 PM–4 PM
LOCATION: 291 Auburn Folsom Road, Auburn
PHONE: 530-305-0048
WEBSITE: www.baumbachwines.com

2 *Lone Buffalo Vineyards*

The Southwest is alive and going strong in the southern portion of Placer County. Lone Buffalo Vineyards, located south of Auburn in the Shirland Tract area, opened its doors in September 2007. The small winery, adjacent to the home of Jill and Phillip Maddux, honors the traditions of the Southwest. It is here, as their owners' catch phrase states, that all are welcomed, "From cowboys to kings."

An avid collector of everything buffalo for the past three decades, Phil, a local attorney, has been making wine even longer. Growing up in Sonoma, Phil had the great fortune of having Sonoma County wine legends Dick Arrowood (Arrowood Vineyards and Winery) and Cecil Deloach (Hook and Ladder Vineyards and Winery) as mentors. He made wine at home and has won countless awards at home winemaker competitions. "Winemaking is his passion and he won't release a wine until he feels it is absolutely ready," said business partner and wife Jill.

The couple has 2 of the nearly 6 acres of their property planted in vines, with another half acre offsite planted with Petite Sirah. According to the duo, "We have a 'down-to-earth' philosophy of winemaking, and our wines are value oriented [which is] so important in today's economy." And naming the winery was a given. "Phil has long admired the buffalo's strength and resilience, so we knew 'buffalo' would figure in our name.

Winery mascot guarding bottles of Lone Buffalo wine

Maintaining a winery demands strength and resilience," explained Jill, who retired from the pharmaceutical industry in 2005 after 25 years. "Who would have ever guessed I'd be doing this now!" she said with a smile.

The Madduxes' winery has a southwestern flare, and the wainscoting was made from the roof of the Blue Goose Fruit Shed. In 1945, the California Fruit Exchange built a fruit packing shed in nearby Loomis at the corner of Taylor and King Roads. Coined the "Blue Goose Fruit Shed," the company shipped Placer County fruit all over the nation. This historic 10,000-square-foot structure is under restoration to make it a major performing arts and event center, and part of the renovation included a new roof. Wanting to keep an important piece of Placer County history in the county, the Madduxes acquired portions of the roof for their tasting room.

The road to Lone Buffalo is private, but, rest assured, winery visitors are welcome. Watch for the speed bumps and please respect the neighborhood by also watching your speed. The winery entrance, marked with a buffalo, is approximately a half mile in and on the right, just before the yellow END road sign.

FEATURED WINES: Syrah, Mourvèdre, and Grenache
TASTING COST: Complimentary
HOURS: Weekends, call for hours
LOCATION: 2682 Burgard Lane, Auburn
PHONE: 916-663-4486
WEBSITE: www.lonebuffalovineyards.com

---

3 *Mt. Vernon Winery*

Found about 2 miles west of Highway 49, Mt. Vernon Winery is Placer County's largest winery. Owned by Lynda and Jim Taylor, who live on the 32-acre estate, the small, picturesque tasting room was originally a milk house for the Semas Ranch, which you'll pass if you come in from Highway 49. (If you're into bull riding, you might enjoy knowing that the ranch was

Courtesy of Mt. Vernon Winery

Mt. Vernon's elegant tasting room

the childhood home of professional bull rider Aaron Semas). According to Lynda, cows used to be milked in the building; far from its humble beginnings, the 60-year-old milk house now offers quality wine and great fun!

The Taylors established their winery in 1996. Son Ryan is their winemaker and an accomplished one at that. According to Lynda, Ryan started making wine when he was only 18; now in his early 30s, he has produced many award-winning wines. In 2007, he worked a harvest in Melbourne, Australia, where he helped put the finishing touches on a Shiraz for Witchmount Estates. It went on to win a gold medal as well as the designation of best Shiraz in the world at the 2008 Syrah du Monde competition in France (www.syrah-du-monde.com).

Of Mt. Vernon's extensive wine list, two are noted for their uniqueness. The first is "Girly Man," named as a result of California's governor Arnold Schwarzenegger's off-handed remark about state legislators. The bottle depicts an almost spot-on caricature of the governor dressed as a caveman and carrying a club. The second is dedicated to helping find a cure for breast cancer. In 2004, Dr. Ernie Boda, creator of the Breast Cancer Research postage stamp, granted the winery exclusive rights to reproduce the stamp on wine labels. Mt. Vernon Winery placed it on their premium wine bottles and donates 12.5 percent for each bottle sold to breast cancer research.

WINE MYTH } **You can lay down wine to age it for 50 years and it just gets better. That is most often going to be vinegar. — Lynda Taylor**

Mt. Vernon's tasting room is absolutely gorgeous. The walls are pieces of art, as grapevines and grapes are done in parget, a French technique involving the use of plaster in decorative style. And the tasting bar has a brass footrail, an unusual attribute for a tasting room.

FEATURED WINES: Zinfandel, Barbera, Syrah, and Cabernet
TASTING COST: Complimentary
HOURS: Thursday–Sunday, 11 AM–5 PM
LOCATION: 10850 Mt. Vernon Road, Auburn
PHONE: 530-823-1111
WEBSITE: www.mtvernonwinery.com

4 *Viña Castellano*

Viña Castellano is a family affair. Established in 1999, the winery is the lifelong dream of Gabriel Mendez, who owns the business with his youngest daughter Teena Wilkins. When asked why they started the winery, Wilkins listed, "to maintain the family estate as a farm, create a generation project, and keep the children off the streets," referring to the family's many children and grandchildren.

Found about 3 miles west of Highway 49 on Bell Road, the 8-acre vineyard and estate is home to many Mendez family members. A stately house stands on a hill and other homes spot the property; hidden to the right is their tasting room, or cave. While a Spanish influence abounds, it is most distinct in Viña Castellano's wines, especially their Tempranillo and Syrah. They also offer a deal on tapas (Spanish appetizers)—if you make advance reservations, they'll have tapas ready when you arrive, at an additional charge. And they host Spanish cave dinners for wine club members in their not-to-be-missed tasting room.

While visiting, walk up the hill to the winery's pond where you'll find a picnic island, referred to as the Tasting Pavilion. According to Wilkins, she and her siblings always wanted their parents to install a built-in pool on the

WINE MYTH } **All wines from Napa are superior.**
           —Teena Wilkins

The tasting pavilion is a picnicker's paradise.

property, but that never happened and the Mendez kids grew up swimming in the large pond instead. While some of the younger Mendez kids still use the pond to cool off, when the winery is open, this beautiful setting, with the vineyard to the right and majestic oaks all around, is strictly for picnicking. Available on a first-come, first-served policy, the picnic table on the island, accessible via a sturdy, rope-lined wooden walkway, is draped with Zinfandel-red curtains and spotted with matching pillows.

FEATURED WINES: Tempranillo and Syrah
TASTING COST: Complimentary
HOURS: Saturday and Sunday, 12 PM–4 PM
LOCATION: 4590 Bell Road, Auburn
PHONE: 530-889-2855
WEBSITE: www.vinacastellano.com

LOOMIS

5 *Secret Ravine Vineyard and Winery*

If Secret Ravine Vineyard and Winery keeps turning out great wines, it won't be a secret much longer! Located in the Loomis Basin area, where more than 150 years ago gold miners worked nearby Secret Ravine Creek in hopes of finding riches, the vineyard and winery is owned by Vicky and Ron Morris. Both are retired from the aerospace industry. In the late 1990s the couple moved to this nearly 5 acres of historic land, learning that from 1870 to 1954, Zinfandel, Tokay, Mataro (Mourvèdre), and Mission grapes could be found here. Today, the couple grows Zinfandel, Syrah, Sauvignon Blanc, Barbera, and Sangiovese on 3 acres of vineyard, with an additional 10 acres of grapes grown on two other properties.

The winery is a family affair, as daughter Renae Messamore helps with facility maintenance and engineering and daughter Melissa Pentoney, business. Not to be outdone, the couple's grandson Chris, who lives with his grandparents and attends junior college, is learning about winemaking. Vicky smiled when she confided that while Chris loves driving the big tractors

A converted horse barn houses the tasting room.

and working the vineyards, their hope is that he will carry on the family business.

Secret Ravine's tasting room is definitely a one-of-a-kind structure. The Morrises spent much time, money, and energy converting the concrete barn and stable into their winery. The tasting room used to be the tack room, and if you get a chance to peek in back, you'll see that stalls have been transformed into barrel and production rooms.

Of their 2,000 cases a year, one fun label is their Rattlesnake Red, which is 85 percent Sangiovese and 15 percent Cabernet Sauvignon. The wine was named for the vineyard on nearby Rattlesnake Bar Road where they purchased their grapes. Eventually, the Morrises started using grapes from their own vineyard, so the rattlesnake name didn't fit—that was, until Vicky came across a huge rattler on their property, which Ron quickly killed. A photograph of the snake now hangs in their tasting room. The legend of Rattlesnake Red lives on!

FEATURED WINES: Sangiovese, Zinfandel, and Sauvignon Blanc
TASTING COST: $5 per person, applied to purchase of six bottles or more
HOURS: Weekends, standard time, 11 AM–4 PM; daylight savings, 12 PM–5 PM
LOCATION: 4390 Gold Trail Way, Loomis
PHONE: 916-652-6015
WEBSITE: www.secretravine.com

NEWCASTLE

6 *Dono dal Cielo Vineyard*

In Italian, *dono dal cielo* means "gift from heaven." Owners Karen and Bill McGillivray believe wholeheartedly in the translation. "We feel this property is a gift from God and we treat it as such. The property came into our life without us looking for it," said Karen.

The locals call the property the Old Ferreira Ranch. In 1932, Domingas and Maria Ferreira owned the land,

A few of the liquid offerings from Dono dal Cielo

naming their home "Rancho Serra da Estrela" after their native Portugal town. For 75 years, the family farmed fresh fruit and dairy products. Eventually, much of Ferreira's property was sold and then subdivided, and the McGillivrays purchased 30 acres of this rich farmland. In 2001, they planted acres upon acres of Zinfandel grapes, using famed root stock from Deaver Vineyards in Amador County. With 6,000 vines planted, these self-described farmers also planted 60 dwarf fruit trees on the property. "Estate farming and processing is our goal. We want a place where people can come and learn and see and smell our family [farm] and winemaking, too," Karen explained, adding that their goal is to establish a friendly, community-oriented atmosphere and business.

This young winery's tasting room is still evolving. The tasting room and winery are combined in a large metal building nestled among the vineyards. Inside, a cozy wine bar greets visitors, and outside, the view is pleasing. And even though they have limited offerings, this winery will, no doubt, gain strength and character as it ages, just like a fine wine. For what it's worth, Dono dal Cielo is definitely heaven sent.

FEATURED WINE: Zinfandel
TASTING COST: Complimentary
HOURS: Saturday and Sunday, 12 PM–4 PM
LOCATION: 6100 Wise Road, Newcastle
PHONE: 530-888-0101
WEBSITE: www.donodalcielo.om

---

7 Ophir Wines

For an outdoor tasting experience, look no further than Ophir Wines. When the weather is gorgeous, owner Paul Burns sets up the tasting room in Mother Nature's backyard. Like camping—where the food always tastes better when you're outdoors—the wine complements the beauty of the vineyard's native oaks and the nearby

WINE MYTH } One true myth is that it takes a lot of beer to make good wine. *—Paul Burns*

View from Ophir's seasonal "outdoor" tasting room

lake, a favorite of local waterfowl (for you bird lovers, a green heron often frequents the lake). Intimate seating can be found throughout, and when a slight chill comes on, Burns warms things up by way of the winery's fire pit. It is truly nature and wine in concert.

Burns said that starting his winery was a culmination of 25 years of winemaking and grape growing by him and two business partners. From planting two vineyards by hand to honing their winemaking skills, the trio introduced their artistic endeavor to the public in 2001, calling their venture Ophir Wines.

Even though their physical address is in Newcastle, the name is for nearby historic Ophir. According to Burns, the town of Ophir was also the location of King Solomon's gold mine, a prominent mine during the great Gold Rush. Because it produced the finest and highest quality gold during that period, Ophir became synonymous with quality. "The name *Ophir* reflects the concept of wine as a blend of people, place, and time," he explained. The winery makes about 1,000 cases annually.

Situated in a quiet valley off the main road, the half-mile drive down a narrow lane passes through a rural residential area, so watch your speed. Once you arrive, you'll find the aforementioned setting (if the weather is cooperative) and a skeleton of a 90-year-old home. If it's not too busy, Burns will show you the vineyard, where he may point out evidence of Chinese surface mining along the perimeter or remnants of the old stone fruit orchards that replaced the mines when the gold ran out. According to Burns, the prized mountain fruit was shipped all over the country.

The goal of Ophir Wines is to create a product that customers will enjoy and talk about. Couple this with their quaint outdoor tasting area, and the threesome have definitely struck gold!

FEATURED WINE: Syrah
TASTING COST: Complimentary
HOURS: Summers, Saturday, 12 PM–5 PM; check website for off-season hours
LOCATION: 7870 Santini Lane, Newcastle
PHONE: 916-531-3055
WEBSITE: www.ophirwines.com

✛ More Area Wineries

LINCOLN

Rancho Roble Vineyards
HOURS: Call for hours
LOCATION: 340 Fleming Road, Lincoln
PHONE: 916-645-2075
WEBSITE: www.ranchoroble.com

SIDE TRIPS

Placer County offers several opportunities for fun side trips. The county seat is **Auburn** (www.old townauburnca.com), located just off Interstate 80, along Highway 49. During the Gold Rush, French immigrant Claude Chana discovered gold in what would become Auburn. To honor this discovery and ultimately the town's creation, Chana is immortalized in a very large concrete statue that is easily seen upon exiting the interstate into the historic district.

Auburn has grown considerably from its Gold Rush days. The stately **Placer County Courthouse,** which is an icon for this notable town, was completed in 1888. Built mostly from local materials, the courthouse bell, a major exception, came around Cape Horn. The building houses the **Placer County Museum** and visitors are welcome. The hill on which the courthouse now sits was once the site of bullfights, bear fights, and public hangings.

On Saturdays at 10 AM, guided tours of historic **Old Town Auburn** originate at the Placer County Museum. The town's motto is "Where history captures your heart," and you'll fall in love with the streets lined by brick buildings filled with quaint shops and eateries. One place of note is the Auburn Ale House. Back in the 1990s, it was the Shanghai Restaurant and Bar; here is where most of the 1996 movie *Phenomenon* was filmed. The movie starred John Travolta, Kyra Sedgwick, Forest Whitaker, and Robert Duvall.

A few miles from Old Town Auburn, heading toward the town of Foresthill on Foresthill Road (via the I-80 exit), you'll cross the **Auburn-Foresthill Bridge,** California's tallest bridge, standing 730 feet above the North Fork of the American River. Pedestrians can walk the 2428 feet of the bridge in both directions. A popular site for BASE jumping, it was here that action star Vin Diesel drove his stolen red Corvette off the side of the bridge in the 2002 movie *xXx,* jumping from the car mid-air and parachuting to his accomplices at the bottom of Auburn Ravine.

The foothill community of Penryn, located 10 miles west of Auburn on I-80, is known not for gold, but for their granite. The **Griffith Quarry Museum** (www.placer.ca.gov/Departments/Facility/Museums/LocalMuseums/quarry.aspx) was once the office of the Penryn Granite Works, established by Welsh immigrant Griffith J. Griffith in 1864. Here he made his fortune and became a regarded philanthropist, purchasing and donating more than 3,000 acres for Los Angeles's Griffith Park. He also donated the money to build the park's Greek Theatre and Griffith Observatory. The museum contains original items from the Griffith family and business, and the first granite polishing mill built in California can be found in the surrounding 23-acre park, even though the mill is now in ruins.

SIDE TRIPS

For More Information

Placer County Wine and Grape Association
4390 Gold Trail Way
Loomis, CA 95650
916-797-WINE (9463)
www.placerwineandgrape.org

Placer Valley Tourism
2204 Plaza Drive
Rocklin, CA 95765
916-773-5400
www.placertourism.com

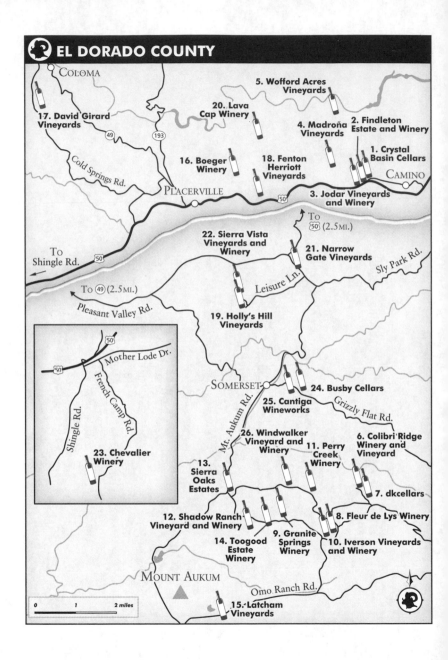

COLOMA

17. David Girard Vineyards

5. Wofford Acres Vineyards

20. Lava Cap Winery

4. Madroña Vineyards

2. Findleton Estate and Winery

1. Crystal Basin Cellars

16. Boeger Winery

18. Fenton Herriott Vineyards

CAMINO

PLACERVILLE

3. Jodar Vineyards and Winery

Cold Springs Rd.

TO 50 (2.5 MI.)

TO Shingle Rd.

22. Sierra Vista Vineyards and Winery

21. Narrow Gate Vineyards

Sly Park Rd.

TO 49 (2.5 MI.)

Leisure Ln.

Pleasant Valley Rd.

19. Holly's Hill Vineyards

Mother Lode Dr.

SOMERSET

24. Busby Cellars

French Camp Rd.

25. Cantiga Wineworks

Grizzly Flat Rd.

26. Windwalker Vineyard and Winery

6. Colibri Ridge Winery and Vineyard

Shingle Rd.

23. Chevalier Winery

13. Sierra Oaks Estates

11. Perry Creek Winery

7. dkcellars

12. Shadow Ranch Vineyard and Winery

8. Fleur de Lys Winery

14. Toogood Estate Winery

9. Granite Springs Winery

10. Iverson Vineyards and Winery

MOUNT AUKUM

Omo Ranch Rd.

0   1   2 miles

15. Latcham Vineyards

★ El Dorado County

E
l Dorado County was one of California's original 27 counties. The county's name is a Spanish term referencing "the gilded man," a king who ruled a land so rich that his body was gilded each morning with a new coating of gold dust. When gold was discovered in Coloma by James Marshall in 1848, the golden riches that lay buried here deserved such a name. While gold previously had been discovered in Southern California, it was the El Dorado County discovery that triggered the Gold Rush.

This area became an important wine region during and after the Gold Rush, with the first vines thought to have been planted in 1849. That first tiny vineyard grew quickly, and by 1859 it was producing between 4,000 and 6,000 gallons of wine each year. Other winery operations, including the Coloma Vineyards and Distillery, which depended on thousands of vines planted on 160 acres near Coloma, were making the owners much more money than gold was making for most miners.

But most of those wineries that survived into the 20th century went out of business during Prohibition. Following the end of Prohibition in 1933, only a few small winery operations returned, as most people believed that the only suitable combination of soils and climate for a successful vineyard was in California's Napa and Sonoma counties.

In 1972, Placerville's old Lombardo-Fossati winery, one of the few that had survived Prohibition 40 years earlier because it was allowed to produce wines for religious organizations, took on a new owner and the Boeger name. Boeger Winery quickly became the largest post–Prohibition winery in the county. By the 1980s, Boeger was producing award-winning Zinfandels and Merlots. A bottle of Boeger's 1980 American Wine Champion Merlot was even presented as a gift by then President Ronald Reagan to the Queen of England, putting El Dorado County wines squarely on the world map of fine wine-producing regions.

CAMINO

1 *Crystal Basin Cellars*

At Crystal Basin, everyone works part-time, and that's okay with them. What began as an amateur cooperative winemaking venture in 1981 has turned into something more. Making their wine at a home in Pollock Pines, the group of newbie winemakers started with three barrels. When their production eventually grew to 25 barrels, the co-op took their hobby commercial in 2000.

"We found that we loved to make wines with our friends and that we have never met a wine grape we didn't like," said Mike Owen, who is founder, president, and "El Jefe." A Silicon Valley escapee, Owen also lived in France for two and a half years where he discovered Rhone wines. "We are the best example of a cooperative winery—run by friends—that was started with a great idea and the change we could find between the cushions of our couches."

Other members of this team include Owen's wife and official Wine Diva, Melissa Owen, who oversees the tasting room and is a natural at handling winery chaos; Peter Zimmerman, winemaker and "Forklift Maestro" who can drive a mean forklift with a kid

Crystal Basin Cellars can be seen from Highway 50.

hanging off each arm; Bill Manson, marketing whiz and "Airplane Guy" who flew here from New England on a wine trip and ended up staying when he realized California lacked humidity; Jack Wohler, "Newly Retired Dude," who helps out and owns a vineyard where he is reaping the benefits of his "alcohol farming"; and "Uncle Bob" Kershaw, the winery's ambassador to France. Melissa's uncle Kershaw is a founding member and works the tasting room. And he's notorious for giving personal tours of the facility; "Be aware," his bio states, "that what happens in the barrel room, stays in the barrel room."

Crystal Basin Cellars can be seen easily from Highway 50 near the Camino exit. Originally a fruit storage facility dating back to 1923, the cellar is insulated by 18-inch-thick walls filled with sawdust from the town's

WINE MYTH } **Syrah/Shiraz came from Persia—horse pucky!**
—Mike Owen

lumber mill. What is striking about this small winery is the vast array of wine offerings, from stunning whites to mouth-watering reds and even port! Crystal Basin is known for their great events, including an annual "Avoid the Malls" gathering they host the Saturday after Thanksgiving. Since the entire staff works part-time, they can live it up every once in a while. "We throw *great* parties!" exclaimed El Jefe Owens.

FEATURED WINES: Cabernet Franc and Mourvèdre
TASTING COST: Complimentary
HOURS: Daily, 11 AM–5 PM (except major holidays)
LOCATION: 3550 Carson Road, Camino
PHONE: 530-647-1767
WEBSITE: www.crystalbasin.com

2 *Findleton Estate and Winery*

"I would rather produce only one high-quality bottle of wine as opposed to a warehouse of ordinary wine," says Tom Findleton, a dedicated winemaker for more than 40 years. Findleton and his wife, nationally recognized artist Pam Findleton, own Findleton Estate and Winery. Their tasting room is located in the Camino Wine Plaza, a small enclave of even smaller wineries perched on a hill next to Highway 50. Findleton's winery anchors the complex, and besides their large tasting room, you'll find relaxing outdoor seating and even a small stage in the pine trees for their many concerts and events.

WINE MYTH } You can make money with a winery. Someone once said, "If you want to make a million in the wine business, start with 10 million!"
—Tom Findleton

A retired general contractor, Findleton was a home winemaker for many years. His reason for going commercial: "We have been passionate winemakers and have appreciated fine wines for more than 30 years now. Quality handcrafted wines produced in the old-world style is the only way to achieve the goal of being able to proudly pour wines that others with a similar passion for wine will appreciate."

Carrie Findleton

Old wine barrels double as wine racks.

The Findletons' vineyard is one of the few in the foothills that produces a Pinot Noir varietal. It's located along Weber Creek, which was named for Captain Charles M. Weber, a member of the Bartleson-Bidwell party who traveled through these parts in 1841 and returned in 1848 with American Indian laborers to search for gold (Weber also founded the city of Stockton). Gold Rush miners bestowed the name "Pneumonia Gulch" on the area in the 1850s and '60s due to the creek's 3000-foot elevation, culminating in warm days and frigid nights. Because of its cold microclimate and rocky volcanic soil, the location is ideal for growing the finicky Pinot Noir grape.

Four generations of Scottish pride help make Findleton wines. Smiling Sam, Tom Findleton's father and head of the clan, relaxes these days while enjoying his favorite wine, Pinot Noir. Tom and Pam's five children are directly involved in the winery; daughter Carrie has a master's degree in viticulture and enology from the University of California at Davis and is a consultant for her family's winery and has interned at many other prestigious wineries around the world; son Kevin, upon interning at two wineries in New Zealand, is assistant winemaker; daughter Jeanetta manages their art and label business; daughter Angela works in the tasting room; and son Tommy works on remodeling their ever-changing winery building. Besides spouses, the rest of clan is comprised of six grandchildren who all help with harvest, crush, music, and food events, and Tom's brother "Lucky" Larry who oversees marketing and web support. Not to be forgotten is "Grizzly," their Australian shepherd vineyard dog; besides chasing away any bird that dares to get too close, Grizzly will greet you in the parking lot and gently guide you into the tasting room.

Pam Findleton is the artist in the family, and her artwork is an integral part of the winery's atmosphere and label branding. Her paintings and work are sought out, and she has pieces on display and for sale at the winery, as well as a combination fine art and wine gallery in nearby Placerville called Fusion Gallery and Findleton Wine Tasting. Located on Main Street, Findleton's newest ventured opened in June 2009. The gallery features more than 20 local artists as well as Findleton wines.

The winery offers free music events from Mother's Day through October, where families are more than welcome. They also give free referrals and "no corking fee" coupons to the area's many restaurants.

FEATURED WINE: Estate-grown Pinot Noir
TASTING COST: Complimentary

MAIN TASTING ROOM
HOURS: Friday–Sunday, 11 AM–5 PM
LOCATION: 3500 Carson Road, Building A, Camino
PHONE: 530-644-4018
WEBSITE: www.finzinwines.com

SECONDARY TASTING ROOM/ART GALLERY
HOURS: Art gallery, Daily, 10 AM–6 PM; tasting room, Thursday–Sunday, 12 PM–6 PM
LOCATION: 440 Main Street, Placerville
PHONE: 530-295-1968
WEBSITE: www.fusionfindleton.com

3 *Jodar Vineyards and Winery*

Even though Jodar Vineyards and Winery is just a hop, skip, and a jump off of Highway 50, loyal customers race to the winery when they get to the exit. If you're smart, you'd follow them to one of the area's most well-regarded wineries.

In production since 1990, the winery was founded by Vaughn and Joni Jodar. While the tasting room is near the highway, via the Carson or Camino Roads exits, the winery is perched 5 miles away, as a crow flies, on Mosquito Ridge. Located at an elevation of 2400 feet, the vineyard literally sits on the edge of the El Dorado National Forest; down a deep chasm below is the South Fork of the American River.

According to Joni, the couple had to use dynamite to blast away giant granite boulders before planting their vineyard. They then planted 4,200 vines on the precipitously carved cliff face. "I think we have the most deeply terraced vineyard in El Dorado County," said Joni. "And we have to use the traditional way of farming since we can't get equipment in there," explaining that because the mountainside is so steep, all of their vineyards are tended by hand, especially during harvest.

WINE MYTH } Winemakers are wizards with mystical powers
of creation. The one with the best grapes gets the
best wine. **—Vaughn Jodar**

Jodar's welcoming tasting room

A registered nurse working in the area, Joni also oversees the tasting room. Husband Vaughn is CEO and winemaker. A former public health advisor with the Centers for Disease Control and Prevention, Vaughn started the winery for an unexpected reason: "Success in another profession evolved into a steady diet of politics," which was not fun, said Vaughn, noting, "When you're pushing 40, it's time for a new life." His foray into the role of winemaker was happenstance. When the winery's original winemaker left in 1999, Vaughn stepped up to the responsibility and won international double gold at Tasters Guild International (www.tastersguild.com) for his very first release, a 1999 Sangiovese.

As with many other Northern California winemakers, Vaughn did get his degree from the University of

California at Davis, but it was in English, not enology. His wines have gone on to become quite well known, including the winery's amazing ports, as well as their first Bordeaux blend called Apollo's Lyre, made from Cabernet Franc, Merlot, and Cabernet Sauvignon.

Over the years, Jodar's tasting room has moved here and there, finally settling in its current location in 2005. Visible from the highway, the comfortable, early California-style building is pleasing, as is the picnic area which overlooks Blakely Lake, just across Carson Road.

FEATURED WINES: Port, Barbera, Cabernet Sauvignon, and a Bordeaux blend
TASTING COST: Complimentary
HOURS: Daily, 11 AM–5 PM
LOCATION: 3405 Carson Court, Camino
PHONE: 530-644-3474
WEBSITE: www.jodarwinery.com

4 *Madroña Vineyards*

Camino is home to Apple Hill, the county's most popular seasonal attraction. Beginning in September, the area is swarming with families craving nearly everything holiday-related, from pumpkins for Halloween to delectable home-grown produce for Thanksgiving and even fresh-cut trees for Christmas. For many, High Hill Ranch is the mecca of this holiday pilgrimage, and that's where you'll find Madroña Vineyards.

Madroña began as vineyards in 1973, with the winery opening in 1980. Given the location's elevation of 3000 feet, owners Dick and Leslie Bush took a chance planting their 32 acres of grapes. But Dick had a hunch that it offered the ideal climate for a vineyard, and he was right, thus making the Bush family noted pioneers in high-elevation vineyards. Today, the family has 200 acres with 67 acres of vineyards planted.

WINE MYTH } Gewürztraminer is originally from Germany.
In fact, it is Italian. —**Maggie Bush**

Madroña Vineyards is named for a large, 300-plus-year-old madrone tree found in the vineyard. According to Maggie Bush, who is married to the couple's son Paul, madrone trees require the same climate and soils as premium grape varieties, noting, "They are not transplantable and grow in a narrow band in El Dorado County, [and

Inside Madroña's large tasting room

are a] great indicator of where grapes will grow well." The tree can be seen to the west as you leave the winery.

Dick and Leslie Bush started Madroña nearly 40 years ago and handed the reins of the business to Paul and Maggie in 2002. Now head winemaker, Paul is acutely aware of the winery's environmental impacts. Madroña is run completely by solar power, and Paul is moving the winery toward sustainable agriculture by using leftovers from the crush process for erosion control in the vineyard.

Nestled beneath towering pines, the tasting room at Madroña is large, and two tasting bars accommodate the many wine lovers who frequent the establishment. Their wine list is huge, and while there are many favorites, one of the more unusual wines is a Gewürztraminer, as the grapes used to make this varietal are not commonly found in this area. Madroña offers complimentary tastings, but there is a $5 charge to taste their reserve wines, with $3 returned when a purchase is made.

The entrance is the driveway for High Hill Ranch, with the winery about three-quarters of a mile in, past the busy ranch. Since the road is one-way only for all who enter, if you visit during the holiday rush, be sure to bring your patience along, too.

FEATURED WINES: Cabernet Franc, Reserve Zinfandel, and Chardonnay
TASTING COST: Complimentary
HOURS: Daily, 11 AM–5 PM
LOCATION: 2560 High Hill Road, Camino
PHONE: 530-644-5948
WEBSITE: www.madronavineyards.com

5 *Wofford Acres Vineyards*

"Come for the wine, stay for the view" is the motto at Wofford Acres Vineyards. The only word for the great view is "spectacular" and it's one of the best out of all of El Dorado County's wineries. Sitting at an elevation of 2541 feet, the winery is perched on a ridge overlooking Redbird Canyon and the South Fork of the American River. There's a large picnic area facing this beautiful vista, with the vineyard right next to it.

Founded in 2003, Wofford Acres is one of the younger wineries in the region, but owner and winemaker Paul Wofford has been making wine for more than 30 years. A California State University at Fresno graduate, Wofford has served as a consultant for just as many years for wineries throughout California. He and his business partners—wife Ann and brother Mike—purchased Cairn Canyon Vineyards and transformed it into their winery.

The Wofford Acres tasting room is rustic, homey, and welcoming, and their wine is popular with locals and visitors alike. Zoe, a broken-coated Jack Russell terrier, is the winery's official greeter, and on weekends she's joined by Mike's yellow Lab "Vi" (as in Viognier). The winery is active in their community; for example, each October, in honor of National Breast Cancer

The amazing view from Wofford Acres Vineyards

Awareness Month, the Wofford family holds a fund-raiser, charging customers to taste certain wines and barrel samples, with proceeds being donated to breast cancer research.

WINE MYTH } The "Wine Country" is Napa Valley only—there are lots of wonderful and diverse California "wine countries." —Ann Wofford

---

Since Wofford Acres Vineyards is off Apple Hill's beaten path, it can sometimes be overlooked. The turn onto Hidden Valley Lane is literally "hidden"—heading west on North Canyon Road, the turn is to the right just before the Hassler Road split. The road looks like a private drive at first glance; continue to the end for that oh-so-terrific view and a winery that is definitely not to be overlooked.

FEATURED WINES: Red blends, including LaMancha
TASTING COST: Complimentary
HOURS: Vary, check website
LOCATION: 1900 Hidden Valley Lane, Camino
PHONE: 888-928-9463 or 530-626-6858
WEBSITE: www.wavwines.com

FAIR PLAY

6 *Colibri Ridge Winery and Vineyard*

Colibri Ridge Winery and Vineyard, located in the eastern reaches of Fair Play and sporting a gorgeous view, is worth the drive. This young winery's friendly staff is excited to pour you some great wines.

Owner John Alexander opened his winery in 2004. Also a winemaker, Alexander was an electronic engineer in his previous life. He began making beer after receiving a kit for Christmas one year, and his curiosity slowly progressed to winemaking. "I planted a pilot vineyard—225 vines—at my residence and made some award-winning wines," Alexander shared. Due to this success, and with the encouragement of neighboring wineries, Alexander opened Colibri Ridge Winery and Vineyard.

When asked about the origins of the winery's name, Alexander explained that *colibri* means "hummingbird" in most European languages. "I like hummingbirds, and [Colibri] sounded much better than 'Hummingbird Hill,'" he said. A popular label is "Rufous Red," named for one of their wine dogs. A large black Labrador retriever, Rufous is featured on the label, sitting in a wine barrel looking up tentatively at a hovering hummingbird. (Rufous is also the name of a

Inside Colibri Ridge's colorful tasting room

species of hummingbird found in California.) Rufous is one of three wine dogs from El Dorado County featured in the fashionable *Wine Dog* series (www.wine dogs.com). Tasting room staff said that Rufous's wine is very popular, as it should be with a celebrity pooch endorsing the product!

The tasting room is inside the barrel room and winery. A small bar is just inside the barn-sized doors, and hummingbird items and wine gifts are available for purchase. Colibri's secluded picnic area is above and to the left of the tasting room among large rock outcroppings and mature oak trees.

Parking is in an upper lot; you can either walk down to the winery on a road around the picnic area or walk along a path through the picnic area. But beware: The path through the picnic area is a little steep, depending on your footwear and physical abilities, so you may want to be dropped off in the lower lot. If you have a valid disabled parking permit, you can park in the small lower lot next to the tasting room's entrance.

FEATURED WINES: Primitivo, Barbera, and White Port
TASTING COST: Complimentary
HOURS: Friday–Sunday, 11 AM–5 PM
LOCATION: 6100 Gray Rock Road, Fair Play
PHONE: 530-620-7255
WEBSITE: www.colibriridge.com

---

7 *dkcellars*

Dave ("d") and Kim ("k") Pratt sold their wine online before opening their tasting room, and the branding and name stuck. The Pratts came to winemaking by accident. Living in Placerville, they were "techies" and had spent years in corporate America, mainly at a cable software company. They found relief from their hectic lives in their own backyard—the wineries of El Dorado County. "Rainy days were made for wine tasting. We'd go to the local wineries and just hang out," said Kim. They became more interested in the winemaking process and began volunteering at wine promotional events and during crush.

Patrons tasting wine at dkcellars

After several years of learning the business, Dave caught the winemaking bug and enrolled in extension courses at the University of California at Davis. In 1997, the Pratts purchased property with an existing 20-year-old vineyard (no winery, though) and named it "Pratt Vineyards." They were grape growers for many years, selling their fruit. In 2000, the Pratts released their first wine, and dkcellars was born.

Farming comes naturally to this very friendly and highly optimistic couple. Kim grew up on a farm, and Dave once lived in the country and worked on a farm. Their motto is "Old world traditions, new world wines." Per Dave, his style of winemaking allows the growing season and vineyard to express itself. "The

Bordeaux are grown, picked, vented, and cellared with the intent of creating a wine that will age for 25 years," he explained. "Our wine is released when it is ready for consumption, not when its predecessor has sold out." While dkcellars best-selling and most critically acclaimed wine is Zinfandel, their passion—and second most critically acclaimed wine—is their Cabernet Sauvignon.

The winery is on Vineyard View Drive, just off of

WINE MYTH } **You cannot make a great Cabernet in the Sierra foothills. —Dave Pratt**

historic Slug Gulch Road. The road was not named after garden slugs, but the road's name was coined during the Gold Rush for a completely different reason. The story goes that a miner was working a riverbed in the area and came across a piece of gold about the size of his thumb. This "slug" was much bigger than a nugget, and when a mine was established at the site, it was named "Slug Gulch Mine."

The Pratts' tasting room is welcoming. "I want customers to feel that they are walking into my kitchen," said Kim. With granite countertops, cherry-wood cabinets, and cork flooring, the style is reminiscent of a gourmet kitchen. Artwork from local artisans lines the walls and is for sale, as are other gift items. And to continue the fun behind the lowercase nouns, dkcellars's wine club is affectionately called the "dkanters." Too clever!

FEATURED WINES: Zinfandel and Cabernet Sauvignon
TASTING COST: Complimentary
HOURS: Friday–Sunday, 11 AM–5 PM
LOCATION: 7380 Vineyard View Drive, Fair Play
PHONE: 530-620-1132
WEBSITE: www.dkcellars.com

---

8 *Fleur de Lys Winery*

The history of Fleur de Lys Winery has a touch of a French love story. Back in the 1960s, in Montreal, Canada, Robert Lajoie lived next door to a girl named Mireille. The two started dating and eventually, after five years, they married. Two weeks after their wedding, the newlyweds left for the U.S. with $600 and their green cards. They ended up in Southern California, purchased a home in Burbank, and found work at a printing company in Pasadena.

A history buff, Robert wanted to visit Coloma's gold discovery site. During their trip to the gold fields, they fell in love with the area. The couple, who had a young daughter at the time, felt that El Dorado County was a much better place to raise her than Southern California; thus, they purchased a

Shayla Seay

A selection of Fleur de Lys's wine

home above Coloma and a small printing company in Placerville.

After 16 years of owning their printing company, Robert and Mireille wanted a change of pace. The Lajoies sold their company and relaxed, enjoying each other's company. Robert loved being outdoors and working with plants, and trips to Napa were frequent getaways, which gave them an idea. With their daughter grown and married, in 1996 they purchased 20 acres in Fair Play, cleared the land, and planted Mourvèdre, Viognier, and Syrah vines. Neighbors encouraged them to open a winery; appreciative of their neighbors' support, the Lajoies purchased another piece of property on Perry Creek Road and opened Fleur de Lys Winery in 2000.

The Lajoies make wine in the French style. Their French-Canadian heritage is evident in their winery's name; *fleur de lys* means "flower of the lily." A prominent insignia, the fleur de lys has appeared on countless European flags and coats of arms, especially that of the French monarchy and in French territories such as Canada. It is also a popular and much used symbol when it comes to ironworks, interior design, and printing.

Fleur de Lys's tasting room is in the winery's barrel room, and their official greeters are dachshunds Frederick Alexander the Grape and Rudolph Valenvino. The mood is French and if you're not careful, you may find yourself feeling romantic due to the ambiance and great wines. More than likely either Robert or Mireille will be pouring from their extensive wine list, which is impressive considering they're a very small winery. And the winery has a very active and large wine club, a testament to their great product and love of making fine wine.

FEATURED WINES: Viognier and Zinfandel
TASTING COST: Complimentary
HOURS: Friday–Sunday, 11 AM–5 PM
LOCATION: 7696 Perry Creek Road, Fair Play
PHONE: 530-620-2246
WEBSITE: www.fleurdelyswinery.com

9 *Granite Springs Winery*

Les and Lynn Russell opened Granite Springs Winery in 1981, only two years after planting their vineyard. They operated the winery until 1994, when Lynn passed away. Close friends and fellow vintners Franklin and Patty Latcham, owners of Latcham Vineyards in nearby Mt. Aukum (see page 115), purchased the business and promised to continue the operation in their friend's name.

Granite Springs was the second vineyard planted in the Fair Play appellation. "There was a modern renaissance of vineyard planting and winery development in El Dorado and Amador counties starting in the late 1970s," explained Margaret Latcham, who now co-owns both wineries with other Latcham family members. "Latcham Vineyards and Granite Springs were two of the original vineyards of the modern era in Fair Play."

As with the majority of wineries and vineyards in the Sierra foothills, history is everywhere. Fair Play was first settled in 1853, and, as the story goes, the town's name arose from an incident in which an appeal for "fair play" deterred a fight between two upset miners. Margaret shared more: "Several European settlers who had come to the Sierra foothills during the Gold Rush were struck by the wonderful climate and soil, which was perfect for cultivating premium wine grapes. The intense heat of the day during the summer gave way to cool

temperatures at night due to the elevation in the foothills. Thus, premium wine grapes could be grown with an exceptional intensity of flavor and depth of character."

Granite Springs was named for the characteristic granite soil and water from deep mineral springs found on its 40 acres, thus giving the wines strength and flavor. Since the winery at Granite Springs is much bigger, wines for both Latcham and Granite are made here, under the watchful eye of winemaker Ruggero Mastroserio. An award-winning winemaker, Mastroserio, who is from Milan, Italy, creates unforgettable varietal wines, as well as terrific dessert wines, including a Petite Sirah Port, Muscat Canelli, and a Black Muscat. Plus, he plays a mean saxophone!

The tasting room at Granite Springs is old-fashioned and charming. Inside you'll find a friendly staff eager to please and a side room that features gourmet food and wine-related gift items. And Granite Springs is famous for having finger foods for their visitors to enjoy with their wine. Outside, you'll find a large pond with a few tables and seating areas that are perfect for picnicking.

FEATURED WINES: Old-clone Zinfandel and Petite Sirah
TASTING COST: Complimentary
HOURS: Saturday and Sunday, 11 AM–5 PM
LOCATION: 5050 Granite Springs Winery Road, Fair Play
PHONE: 800-638-6041 or 530-620-6395
WEBSITE: www.latcham.com

Granite Springs's signature label features the California quail.

10 *Iverson Vineyards and Winery*

Since Iverson Vineyards and Winery opened their doors to the public in March 2007, owners Mike and Melodie "D" Iverson have never looked back. They had finally realized their dream of owning a winery.

In 1977, the Iversons moved from the Bay Area to the foothills to work for California ISO (Independent System Operator), a nonprofit public-benefit corporation charged with operating the majority of California's high-voltage wholesale power grid. Mike was manager of operations, and Melodie worked in the finance department. The couple began wine tasting in the foothills and discovered and fell in love with the Fair Play region.

Needing a break from their stressful corporate lives, and desiring something they would enjoy doing together, they decided to open a winery. The Iversons spent three years learning all they could, and in 2000 purchased 32 acres and began a seven-year project of planting vines and building their winery and tasting room. Mike retired in 2005 to run the business, and Melodie is hoping to retire soon.

For the Iversons, it's all about the wine; they firmly believe wine should be a part of everyday life, not reserved for special events. They also feel that a great wine enhances a cozy dinner at home or a festive gathering

Iverson Vineyards's pristine tasting room

with friends and family. The winery produces fewer than 3,000 cases annually, limiting their production so that they may focus on making high-quality wine. They have 8 acres of vineyard, made up of Primitivo, Barbera, Merlot, Cabernet Sauvignon, Sangiovese, Petite Sirah, Zinfandel, Cabernet Franc, and Malbec.

Because Iverson is such a small operation, friends and family members help out during special events. If you attend one of their many wonderful wine affairs, don't be surprised if you see *two* Melodies! Owner Melodie has two sisters, and one—Melanie Duensing of Chico, California—is her twin. During these events, Melanie works the tasting room and Melodie works in the event area. "Most people who know Melodie get a little confused when they first see her sister and do not get their usual greeting," laughed Mike. It's when they see another Melodie in the event area that they realize there are two of them. "The sisters seem to have a lot of fun with this 'twins' thing," he explained. Another form of entertainment for the Iversons is taking off on their Harley Davidson to explore with a bottle of their wine, of course, and picnic goodies in their saddlebag!

"Life is good," said Mike. And why shouldn't it be? The couple has a gorgeous home on a knoll just 400 feet from the tasting room. They have spent countless hours attending to every detail of their new business, and it shows. Their tasting room is pristine, polished, and absolutely fabulous! If you're a shopper, you'll be delighted by the gourmet items and one-of-a-kind gifts for sale. On the front veranda, you can relax in a white wicker chair and gaze out over their vineyard or wander over to their large granite patio where you'll find seating areas to enjoy a picnic. The impressive, expansive view of the foothills might make you daydream about one day owning a winery yourself!

FEATURED WINES: Sauvignon Blanc, Barbera, and Merlot
TASTING COST: Complimentary
HOURS: Thursday–Monday, 11 AM–5 PM
LOCATION: 8061 Perry Creek Road, Fair Play
PHONE: 530-620-7474
WEBSITE: www.iversonwinery.com

11 *Perry Creek Winery*

Perry Creek Winery, one of the first wineries in Fair Play, is known for their Zinfandels. Their flagship wine, ZinMan Zinfandel, is so popular that the name is a registered trademark. Perry Creek's 2006 ZinMan received 86 points (out of a possible 100) from *Wine Spectator* in fall 2008.

The back label reads: "The legend of the ZinMan can be traced all the way back to the days of the Gold Rush. It was then that reports first trickled in about a mystical creature known to sprinkle ZinDust upon the high-altitude vines of the Sierra Foothills. Over 150 years later, the fruits of his labors can be experienced in bottles of ZinMan wine, infused with ZinDust and the magical flavors that make up Perry Creek Wines."

Another prominent wine is Perry Creek's Altitude: 2401 label. Considered their reserve wines, the Altitude series is named, appropriately, for the elevation of the vineyard. The 2005 Altitude: 2401 Petite Sirah was named the best Petite Sirah at the 2008 California State Fair wine competition. Then there's the CobraZin label, with a red cobra arched in a striking position, fangs exposed. "This is a fun label we made at the owner's request. He owns a red AC Cobra," shared winemaker Joe Flemate, referring to a line of British-built and -designed sports cars produced in the 1960s.

Shayla Seay

Perry Creek's mission-style tasting room

Michael Chazen opened Perry Creek in 1989. In 2006, he sold the winery to Dieter Jurgens, the owner of that red AC Cobra. Named for a small creek in the area, the winery and its tasting room are reminiscent of the California mission–style and include a fun gift boutique. Outside, you can sit on the veranda or picnic under the pines.

FEATURED WINES: Zinfandel, Syrah, Petite Sirah, and Viognier
TASTING COST: Complimentary
HOURS: Daily, 11 AM–5 PM
LOCATION: 7400 Perry Creek Road, Fair Play
PHONE: 530-620-5175
WEBSITE: www.perrycreek.com

12 *Shadow Ranch Vineyard and Winery*

Shadow Ranch Vineyard and Winery is one of the newer additions to Fair Play's successful wine region, and they feature a varietal that is uncommon for this area—Sauvignon Blanc. White wine lovers, rejoice!

Kimari and Sam Patterson purchased 80 gorgeous acres, tucked behind a hill just off of Fair Play Road, in 2006, and opened the winery in July 2007. A graduate of the University of California at Davis, Sam had vast experience as a viticulturist and vineyard manager in Napa Valley and Amador and El Dorado counties, before opening his winery. For him, planting his 7.5 acres of Sauvignon Blanc was the easy part. "I have no intention of planting 80 acres of grapes. In reality, if we planted another 7 acres, that would be all. I do want to get some Zinfandel in the ground," Sam said, adding that everything is farmed organically, using renewable energy. To learn more about Sam, read his winemaker interview at **www.WineOhGuide.com.**

Once a large, working cattle ranch, many of the property's original buildings are still intact and evident as you drive into the winery. While some of these buildings are used for storage, the main house—built in 1888—doubles as the tasting room. It features a stunning walnut bar and is inside what used to be the living room. Sam's father is a master carpenter, and his superb craftsmanship is evident in this building and the barrel room. The rest of the house

Authors' son Shawn cracking walnuts at Shadow Ranch

is used for offices and storage; a large room in the back doubles as a meeting and special events space.

In the tasting room you'll find a basket of walnuts from the property's orchard (which includes fig trees) and a walnut cracker mounted to the top of an old wine barrel outside. When asked if the cracker was a big draw for the kids, Sam laughed: "We have a rule for children; anything they open, they have to eat. That's pretty much eliminated my daughter from using that machine. She's five years old, and my son will be two next month."

The couple's daughter likes to help at the winery, as does Sam's nephew, who, at age eight, is big enough to help punch-down the fermentation vats. When asked about Kimari's role in the winery, Sam bragged about his wife: "She's our resident artist. We make primarily everything that we sell here, such as the candles. She's a goldsmith by trade. She makes all the jewelry we sell in the tasting room. She does all of our special event coordination and works the tasting room a few days each week. And she does a fabulous job raising our two children."

The winery, which has shaded picnic areas, is a great place to kick back, relax, and enjoy the view, with a refreshing bottle of Shadow Ranch wine, of course!

FEATURED WINE: Sauvignon Blanc
TASTING COST: Complimentary
HOURS: Thursday–Sunday, 11 AM–5 PM
LOCATION: 7050 Fair Play Road, Fair Play
PHONE: 530-620-2785
WEBSITE: www.shadowranchwinery.com

13 *Sierra Oaks Estates*

As with many of the foothills wineries, Sierra Oaks Estates began as a passion. Owners Jim Brown and his wife Toshi became interested in wine in the early 1970s when they lived in Marin County. They loved visiting the nearby wineries in Sonoma and Napa, but nothing prepared them for when Jim tried making wine himself. His first wine, made using a kit, came out much better than the cheaper wines they purchased from the store. Jim's interest soon became a full-fledged hobby, and he continued making wine at home for several years.

The couple formed a wine tasting club in the Bay Area; each month, the club tasted different wines, and trips to wine regions were organized annually. Needless to say, the Browns' wine knowledge and related activities improved Jim's winemaking skills.

On one of those club trips, the couple discovered the Sierra foothills. Close to retirement from the corporate world, they dreamed of starting their own vineyard. Returning to the foothills, they purchased 40 unimproved acres in 1994 and prepared the land for planting, but it wasn't as easy as sticking a vine in the ground. Still living in Marin County, the couple toiled each and every weekend and during their vacation time

WINE MYTH } **Great wine has to be aged 10 years.**
—Jim Brown

Shawn Shiflet

Sierra Oaks's gift shop and art gallery

to dig a well, install irrigation pipes, put in a road, and build a barn. By July 1995, they had planted 3 acres of Merlot, adding another 1.5 acres the following year.

Two years later, the couple retired and moved to their foothill retreat. They planted more vineyards, and with Jim's winemaking expertise improving, they decided to go commercial. The Browns opened Sierra Oaks Estates in 2001 with just one wine, a Merlot. But that same year, the couple had a bumper crop of Merlot, and Jim made a full line of wines, including an estate Merlot made in several styles, an estate Rose made from Merlot, and an estate Syrah.

As any great winemaker should be, Jim is picky about his primary ingredient. "We take great care to be sure the grapes are properly grown and are ripe to our specifications, making a well-balanced, nicely structured wine, with great mid-palate fruit," he explained. His reputation precedes him as he is a sought-after wine consultant at other area wineries.

You can taste Brown's award-winning wines for yourself at his tasting room, located on the corner of Mt. Aukum and Fair Play roads. An art gallery, featuring local artists, adds to the flavor and fullness of the wine and the ambiance of the tasting room.

FEATURED WINES: Zinfandel and Barbera blend called Zinzabar
TASTING COST: Complimentary
HOURS: Wednesday–Sunday, 11 AM–5 PM
LOCATION: 6713 Mt. Aukum Road, Fair Play
PHONE: 530-620-7079
WEBSITE: www.sierraoaksestates.com

14 *Toogood Estate Winery*

Toogood Estate Winery is known for many things, the most popular of which is its "cave" tasting room. Entering the built-in, H-shaped wine cave is a treat; walking along a softly lit passageway lined with wine barrels, you'll soon find yourself in their tasting room. This is a wonderful place to be on a hot day, as the instant drop in temperature will make your visit that much more enjoyable.

Owning a winery was a long-time dream for Paul Toogood. Born and raised in Southern California, Toogood is somewhat of a Renaissance man. A champion swimmer in the early 1970s, he ranked sixth in the world in the butterfly, which earned him a scholarship to Cornell University. There he obtained an undergraduate degree in animal science and biology, and then finished his schooling at the University of California at Davis, earning a degree in veterinary medicine and a minor in viticulture and enology. He opened a veterinary practice in Yuba City, a career that has now spanned three decades.

In 2001, his desire to open a winery culminated in his purchasing 40 acres in Fair Play. Considering the layout of the land, which included a large hill, Toogood envisioned a massive wine cave. He hired engineers to advise him on how to proceed; they said it would be impossible. Toogood wouldn't hear of it. Determined to have his cave, excavation began on September 11,

Entrance to Toogood's famed wine cave

2001. After nine months of dedication, hard work, and sheer resolve, Toogood's dream became a reality—he finally had his wine cave.

Toogood Estate's 5,000-square-foot wine cave stays at a constant 61°F with steady humidity year-round. These two factors, combined with the cave's darkness, culminate in near-perfect conditions for aging wine slowly and evenly. The estate's first crush took place in 2002, with the wine being bottled and sold in 2003. Toogood's winemaker is the legendary Marco Cappelli; also a consultant, Cappelli is responsible for many superb wines coming from myriad wineries in this region.

Toogood Estate's 12 acres of vineyards include the varietals Zinfandel, Primitivo, Tempranillo, Pinot Noir,

Merlot, Cabernet Franc, and Petite Sirah. Their signature wine, Foreplay, is a provocative Bordeaux blend.
Other labels have names you might expect from a veteri-
narian: Red Mutt and Rocket Dog Red. The estate also
features a private Grand Cave dining room that can be
reserved for a unique tasting or dining experience, and
winery staff can assist in the selection of a caterer.

FEATURED WINES: Zinfandel, Primitivo, Petite Sirah, and Tempranillo
TASTING COST: $5 per person
HOURS: Daily, 11 AM–5:30 PM
LOCATION: 7280 Fair Play Road, Fair Play
PHONE: 530-620-1910
WEBSITE: www.toogoodwinery.com

MOUNT AUKUM

15 Latcham Vineyards

Latcham Vineyards, located in southern El Dorado
County, is the heart and soul of winemaking in this
region. The Latcham name is synonymous with quality and distinction, as is evident by their reputation in
the industry.

Franklin Latcham and his wife Patty moved to Mt.
Aukum in the early 1980s with their four children. Prior
to the move, Latcham spent 50 years as a tax attorney

for Morrison and Foerster, one of San Francisco's oldest law firms, established in 1892. During his five decades as an attorney, he met and married Patty, the first female attorney hired by the Federal Reserve; taught law at Yale; created the law field "State and Local Taxation" and wrote the very first law journal for this field; became head of the Morrison and Foerster's tax branch; and was very instrumental in the firm's hiring of women and minority attorneys. Latcham also went before the U.S. Supreme Court many times, winning the majority of his cases before that honored court.

WINE MYTH } Wine should be elitist and snobby and intimidating.
—Margaret Latcham

Being romantic and wanting to learn new things led both him and Patty to the wine industry. They had enjoyed wine tasting in Napa and Sonoma, so they started searching for property in that area to start their winery. Then a trip in the early 1980s to El Dorado County and Boeger Winery—practically the only winery in the region at the time—changed their minds. Cofounder and winery patriarch Greg Boeger told them they should buy their land in the foothills instead and help develop a new wine region.

Intrigued by Boeger's pioneering idea, and also by their love of history and the Gold Rush era, the Latchams bought land in Mt. Aukum and planted a vineyard. Latcham Vineyards was the fourth vineyard to be planted

Some of Latcham's award-winning wines

in the Fair Play AVA, and for nearly a decade, the Lat-chams sold their grapes to other wineries. Keeping his day job, Frank made the commute from San Francisco to Mt. Aukum when he could, finally retiring in 1990.

With Frank's retirement, the family decided to cre-ate their own wine under their own label. According to daughter Margaret Latcham, coming up with a name for the winery was not easy: "Actually, my mother suggested that we use our own family name for our winery. My father and I were looking through several collections of wine labels one day. There were numerous labels featur-ing animals, mountains, lakes, and natural formations. Finally, my mom said, 'Why don't we call our winery Lat-cham Vineyards? The name will be distinctive, and since we are proud of our product, we should have the gumption to put our name on the label!'" She won her case.

Latcham wines are made at their other winery—Granite Springs Winery in Fair Play (see page 99). Up until his passing in August 2008 at age 86, Frank Latcham was very active in the family business. Now Margaret and her brother Jon run both wineries, and mother Patty and two other brothers are partners. "The good part of working with family members is an ease and familiarity of purpose and communication," shared Margaret.

The winemaker for both Latcham and Granite Springs is Ruggero Mastroserio. From Milan, Italy, he believes in making wines that respect the varietal characteristics of the grapes from which they are made. As Margaret said, "Ruggero's passion is to create wines that are as rich and as deeply flavorful as possible."

Flavor is what you get when you taste a Latcham wine—no wimpy wines for this family! Confident Zinfandels, daring Barberas, and terrific port wines pair perfectly with Margaret's "Pass the Port" brownies, which are always on the counter (and they're FREE!). Gooey and decadent, these to-die-for brownies have a cult following among wine lovers. One bite, with a sip of a Latcham wine, and you'll never look at another brownie the same way again. You can pick up a copy of the recipe at the winery or at **www.WineOhGuide.com.**

Latcham's tasting room is in a large barn-style building overlooking a portion of the vineyard. The staff is friendly, exuberant, and very knowledgeable. On warm days and during special events, the Latchams throw open the big barn door. The bar is more than 20 feet long to accommodate tasters, and the place is always busy. Outside you'll find a beautiful picnic area, along with a cat or two to keep you company.

FEATURED WINES: Old-clone Zinfandel, Barbera, and Cabernet Franc
TASTING COST: Complimentary
HOURS: Thursday–Monday, 11 AM–5 PM
LOCATION: 2860 Omo Ranch Road, Mt. Aukum
PHONE: 800-750-5591 or 530-620-6642
WEBSITE: www.latcham.com

PLACERVILLE

16 *Boeger Winery*

The Boeger family has been in the wine business since 1890. Family patriarch Anton Nichelini, a Swiss-Italian immigrant, came for the Gold Rush but stayed for the agricultural gold, settling in Napa County. His winery still exists; found in the Chiles Valley, Nichelini Winery is the oldest, continuously family-operated winery in Napa County.

Nichelini's grandson is Greg Boeger, who, with his wife Sue, founded El Dorado County's Boeger Winery in 1972. But they didn't start completely from scratch:

The couple purchased a 1860s Gold Rush–era vineyard and winery once owed by the Lombardo-Fossati family, turning it into the county's first modern winery and the first one to open following Prohibition. The Boegers poured their wine from the historic 1860s cellar for years until building their drop-dead gorgeous tasting facility just up the hill.

The historic cellar, with the original home on the second level, is now used for special events and over-flow tasting. The structure is the first building you'll pass on the way to Boeger's larger tasting room. And as you drive by, you'll go under a Mission grapevine that stretches across the road and along the home's balcony. This vine is one of the few remaining original vines found on the grounds. During Prohibition, the Fossati family was allowed to produce small amounts of sacramental wine for a local church and personal use. Unfortunately, due to Prohibition (1920–1933) most of the vineyard was pulled out and converted to pear orchards. The Fossatis were quite successful with their orchards until disease wreaked havoc throughout the entire region; in 1972, the land was sold to the Boegers who then planted their vineyards.

Talking with Greg Boeger, it becomes obvious that his blood runs red with wine and that he is passionate about his craft. Much of his childhood was spent at his grandfather's winery, so following in his grandfather's footsteps was a natural calling. But there was just one twist: "After graduating from Davis in 1967, I wanted to grow grapes and make wine on my own *outside* of the Napa Valley," Boeger said. The foothills called to him and to his sense of innovation. Now considered nationally a master winemaker, Boeger took a chance when starting out by planting Merlot (1978) and Barbera (1982)—both of which were virtually unheard of in California at that time. His introduction of these two now extremely prominent varietals resulted in a Merlot so remarkable that it was served in the White House during President Ronald Reagan's administration. According to Greg, this single event revolutionized the Golden State's wine industry and put Boeger Winery on the map.

WINE MYTH } Owning a vineyard and winery is a leisure and aristocratic life, like we ride a white horse through the vineyards daily. In reality, it is farming, hard work, and a gamble with Mother Nature and the wine market. **—Greg Boeger**

From their first vintage in 1972, which resulted in 500 bottles, to today's output of 22,000 cases annually, Boeger Winery hosts 38 varietals in seven vineyards. The two prominent vineyards visible on-site are the Estate and Fossati Vineyards. Combined, the vineyards equal 40 acres (Boeger has another five vineyards offsite, totaling another 50 acres). The Estate Vineyard, which surrounds the winery, is the one planted by Boeger back in 1973 and is the site of the original 1870s vineyard of Giovanni Lombardo. The Fossati Vineyard can been seen at the

Lombardo-Fossati historic cellar and home, built circa 1860

winery's entrance and is contiguous with the Estate Vineyard. Boeger's son Justin spearheaded the conversion of the aging pear orchard to a vineyard in 1998, planting many varietals including Zinfandel, which was propagated from the old vines that had survived from the 1880s. Boeger's Old Clone Zinfandel comes from this vineyard.

In 2002, after 30 years of winemaking, Greg turned over this responsibility to son Justin. A University of California at Davis enology graduate who interned in Germany, Justin is creating a new generation of Boeger wine (to learn more about Justin, read his winemaker interview at **www.WineOhGuide.com**). This award-winning winemaker pulls double duty as the head wine-maker at Nichelini Winery as well, just like his great-grandfather did more than 150 years ago.

Boeger's tasting room is stylish, yet rustic. Besides tasting from their extensive wine list, where the first six tastes are complimentary, the winery also sells gourmet items and picnic supplies. The grounds are a real treat and the Boegers encourage picnicking either under redwoods that line a bubbling creek and pond or in the winery's historic orchard. And if you look around the grounds, you'll find whimsical treats such as a sign that states UNATTENDED CHILDREN WILL BE GIVEN CANDY AND A FREE PUPPY.

History is everywhere, from the small collection of antique cars and trucks Greg is presently restoring to a curious piece of history imprinted in the old cellar's door. Here you'll find the federal tax stamp that served as the license to distill spirits before the Eighteenth Amendment put an end to the production of alcohol. Next to the cellar is an ancient fig tree, and up on the hill is an old barn structure that was the original distillery for making brandy.

FEATURED WINES: Barbera and Zinfandel
TASTING COST: First six tastes are complimentary
HOURS: Daily, 10 AM–5 PM
LOCATION: 1709 Carson Road, Placerville
PHONE: 530-622-8094
WEBSITE: www.boegerwinery.com

17 *David Girard Vineyards*

David Girard Vineyards is a wine lover's paradise found. From the meandering drive through the oak-laden grounds past vineyard after vineyard, settling into a serene valley with a quiet lake and stunning villa-style winery, you'll think you're in France, even though you're less than a mile away from the spot where James Marshall discovered gold.

At an elevation of 1300 feet, the soils and microclimate found at David Girard are akin to that of the south of France. David Girard's 85 acres of vineyard property also hosts mature fruit trees similar to those found in France's Rhone Valley. The Rhone style of wines is the heart of the winery's offerings, even though they feature other varietals as well.

The winery is owned by attorney David Girard. Girard grew up just outside of Detroit; at that time, his loves were hockey, snow, and the automotive industry, and during high school and college, he worked at his father's gas station. Fast-forward through a stint in the U.S. Army and a few other odd jobs, Girard earned his M.B.A. and then a law degree from the University of Michigan.

Now with a wife and daughter, he headed to the University of California at Berkeley where he earned his Ph.D. and practiced law for a while. Girard then moved to Europe for a year, returning to teach educa-

David Girard's elegant winery and tasting room

tional finance at the University of California at Santa Barbara and then at his alma mater in Berkeley. During that time, the couple had another daughter. Eventually, Girard returned to practicing law, representing schools and colleges.

It wasn't until 1992 that Girard purchased the Placerville property and planted his vineyard. "The truth is it just *seemed* like it would be fun. Who knew it would be so much work?" said Girard. "We initially grew grapes for Mondavi. Then we decided we might be able to make some fairly decent wines ourselves. I think we have."

Mari Wells, who used to be with Chatom Vineyards in Calaveras County, is Girard's winemaker. Well regarded by other winemakers in the industry, Wells originally wanted to be a sea captain like her father, even enrolling in the California Maritime Academy. "We call her 'Captain' or 'The Little General,'" said Girard. "She is funny, competitive, passionate, and a damn good winemaker." (To learn more about Wells, read her interview at **www. WineOhGuide.com**). For those who like to learn about what they're drinking, the winery offers a fact sheet on their website for each current release, with technical annotations, such as alcohol listing and blend composition, and winemaker notes from Wells, too.

WINE MYTH } Wine tasting is an intimidating, complicated, pretentious process. I like Robert Mondavi's philosophy: If you like it, it's good; if you don't, it's bad.
—David Girard

Wells's fantastic wines are the focus of Girard's tasting room. Classic and relaxed, the tasting area reflects Girard's unpretentious style. As he puts it himself, his winery is "small and unhurried." Girard strongly encourages visitors to partake in the waterfall terrace and walk the grounds, like he does when his grandkids visit. "I love to walk the [vineyard] rows holding my grandchildren's hands."

As noted earlier, David Girard Vineyards is just a mile uphill from Marshall Gold Discovery State Historic Park, in the historic town of Coloma. It was here that gold was first discovered in 1848, sparking the great Gold Rush. To learn more, see "Side Trips" (page 164). If you're a history buff, here's a scoop: You'll find the historic Coloma Cemetery less than a mile down Cold Springs Road, right before Highway 49. It's a quick turn to the right, so watch for it as you near the bottom of the hill. Here you'll find notable headstones and grave markers of the area's pioneers, so be sure to take your camera with you.

Even closer to David Girard is the site of the Wakamatsu Tea and Silk Farm Colony, the first agricultural settlement of Japanese immigrants in North America, which was settled in 1869. The grave of resident Okisan is about all that is left, and it's on private property. The American River Conservancy does give periodic group tours (for reservations, call 530-295-2190). A historic marker can be found on the grounds of Gold Trail Union Elementary on Cold Springs Road. If you visit during school hours, for security reasons, park in the school's front lot and check in at the office before heading to the marker.

FEATURED WINES: Syrah, Mourvèdre, Grenache, and Viognier
TASTING COST: Complimentary
HOURS: Thursday–Sunday, 11 AM–5 PM
LOCATION: 741 Cold Springs Road, Placerville
PHONE: 530-295-1833
WEBSITE: www.davidgirardvineyards.com

18 *Fenton Herriott Vineyards*

 Owner and winemaker Guy Herriott is the heart and soul behind Fenton Herriott Vineyards. It's obvious where the Herriott in the winery's name comes from, but the Fenton nomenclature is a little trickier to figure out: According to Herriott, Fenton is his grandfather's middle name. "I chose the name because I wanted a family name and something that was a bit different," explained Herriott. "His full name was Donald Fenton Herriott and I thought that 'Fenton Herriott' had a nice ring to it."

For such a small winery, Fenton Herriott makes a remarkable number of wines. With a dozen choices on their tasting list at any given time, the more unusual for this area include a Rose and a Gewürztraminer. And their offerings are so popular that the winery sometimes sells out, hence the construction of a new building, nestled into a hillside on the way to the tasting room. "The new winery was built here to take advantage of the natural cooling effect of the ground, which provides a constant temperature year-round without the need for electricity," Herriott explained. He also shared that plans are in the works to install solar panels, making Fenton Herriott a nearly electricity-free operation, "This will be my small part to help fight climate change, and it will allow the winery to continue

Entrance to Fenton Herriott's tasting room

to grow and make even more of the wines people have come to love."

For Herriott, winemaking was happenstance. Employed full-time as a software engineer at Hewlett-Packard, he was also working toward his master's degree in software engineering at Sacramento State University. Needless to say, he was a busy guy. Graduating in 1999, suddenly Herriott had extra time on his hands; to fill the void, he began making wine, learning the craft from local home winemakers. Discovering his passion, Herriott took enology and vineyard management courses at the University of California at Davis. In 2001, he purchased the current property and built his winery. His first two vintages, a Barbera and a Syrah, were released in 2003.

WINE MYTH } **A winery must be known for a particular wine.**
   —Guy Herriott

The winery is located on Jacquier Road, between Carson Road to the north and Smith Flat Road to the south. Besides the inviting tasting room, the winery has a huge gazebo with comfortable chairs and tables for picnicking, all of which overlook the winery's vineyard and gardens. There are also two bocce ball courts for playing a game or two, and if you absolutely need to check your e-mail, they have Wi-Fi access.

FEATURED WINES: Rose, Gewürztraminer, Sangiovese, Barbera, White Port, and Syrah
TASTING COST: Complimentary
HOURS: Daily, 11 AM–5 PM
LOCATION: 120 Jacquier Court, Placerville
PHONE: 530-642-2021
WEBSITE: www.fentonherriott.com

---

19 *Holly's Hill Vineyards*

Carrie and Josh Bendick are in their early thirties. Now that might not be sensational, but they're reminded of their age quite often when people exclaim that they're just too young to be winemakers. "It's the same reaction every time," said Carrie, who shares winemaking responsibilities at Holly's Hill Vineyards with her husband Josh. "Most people feel that a winemaker should be some little old man."

In tasting the wine at Holly's Hill, you would think that the Bendicks have been making wine all of their lives. Their offerings are delicious, including their estate Rhone red blend called Patriarche. According to Carrie, the winery releases a different vintage of Patriarche every year, noting they use a different blend each time. "We take the best representation of what we grew that year and put it together in the crusher. This produces a more cohesive wine. We'll add individual fermented wines until the blend is just right."

Carrie and Josh met in 1998 through a mutual friend during the Amador County Fair wine tasting event. At the time, Carrie was pouring wine for Somerset's Windwalker Winery, and Josh was doing the same for Boeger Winery, where he worked. Soon after that meeting, Josh invited Carrie to a surprise party for the friend who introduced him. Carrie confided that after five minutes on the phone with Josh, she knew she would marry him. The couple wed seven months later and now have three daughters, age five and younger. "The girls help during harvest," said Carrie. "They're still a little young, but they love it!"

WINE MYTH } **All winemakers are little old men.**
    —Carrie Bendick

Holly's Hill Vineyards harvested their first crop in 2000. Located in the Pleasant Valley region, their 25 acres of vineyards are steeply terraced with a variety of Rhone grapes. You can see the layout on their website; a photo shows the contents of the entire hillside, looking east from the top of the Syrah vineyard. Because the vineyards are planted in a circular-oriented fashion, the grapes receive 360-degree exposure to the sun.

Carrie's parents, Tom and Holly Cooper, are the winery's owners. It's obvious that the winery is named after Holly, who, per her daughter, was the driving force behind the purchase of the original vineyard property. Holly also had some help from dear friend and college

Inside the tasting room at Holly's Hill

roommate Mary Pash. As you walk up the pathway to the tasting room, look to your left; you'll see a small sign with Pash's name on it. Pash was diagnosed with a brain tumor and when she died in 2003, she left her dear friend money in her will, which came as a complete surprise to Holly. To honor Pash, Holly used the money to plant a vineyard of Counoise, a Rhone varietal not commonly grown in California.

As you might expect, the winery's tasting room is perched on top of Holly's Hill, overlooking the vast Cosumnes River valley. It has open beam construction and gorgeous, rustic wood flooring, with a large deck. More than likely you'll run into Drake, the winery dog, who will welcome you to his domain. And if you're a blog fanatic, check out Josh's blog, appropriately entitled "Only the Rhonely" (http://hollyshill.blogspot.com). While tasting is complimentary, there is a $5 charge to taste from their reserve list, which can be applied toward a purchase.

FEATURED WINES: Mourvèdre, Grenache, and Viognier
TASTING COST: Complimentary
HOURS: Daily, 10 AM–5 PM
LOCATION: 3680 Leisure Lane, Placerville
PHONE: 530-344-0227
WEBSITE: www.hollyshill.com

---

20 *Lava Cap Winery*

Lava Cap Winery can thank the miners of 1849 for their name. David Jones, a geology professor and Lava Cap's owner, likes to tell the story: "During the time period from 4 to 10 million years ago, high volcanoes flared up along the eastern Sierra Nevada. Volcanic flows of lava, ash, and debris poured down and covered most of the Sierra's western slope. Most of this volcanic layer has weathered away, but it is still found in a few special places in the foothills. The 49er miners discovered that rich gold deposits lay under this volcanic layer of rock. They called it the 'lava cap.'"

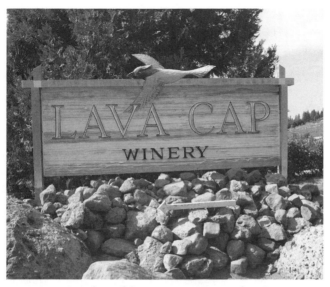

Lava Cap's beautiful sign greets visitors to the winery.

David and his wife Jeanne started making wine as a hobby, planting two rows of Cabernet Sauvignon in their San Francisco Peninsula backyard. Their hobby grew, and in the early '80s, the couple purchased land in Placerville and planted a much larger vineyard, working toward their goal of opening a winery. In 1986, Lava Cap Winery became a reality and a family affair, as their two boys, Tom and Charlie, play an important role in the business, as winemaker and vineyard manager, respectively.

Tom earned his master's degree in enology from the University of California at Davis, which, per Jeanne, provided a wonderful scientific framework for creating his wines. "The artistic side of his endeavor is largely self-taught via continuous experimentation, observation, and curiosity," said Jeanne, noting that her son enjoys creating things from metal and wood.

WINE MYTH } A myth about wine is that you need to be a "connoisseur" to enjoy it. The best way to know about wine is to try different wines and discover what pleases you. What makes wines so interesting is the great variety of flavors and how they blend with food or just taste good to sip on their own. **—Jeanne Jones**

Charlie is a man of the land. His favorite aspect of growing Lava Cap grapes is the unique combination of growing conditions. "The 2400- to 2700-foot elevation keeps us above the valley and coastal fog and ensures lots of sunshine to fully ripen the grapes," he noted. "The nighttime air flow down the vineyard valley to the American River Canyon keeps the grapes cool in hot weather and prevents frost damage in the early spring." Add this unique microclimate to the vineyard's lava cap, and the results are wines with intense flavors and distinctive complexity.

Lava Cap is one of the most decorated wineries in the El Dorado appellation. The majority of their wine list is red varietals, with their Petite Sirah being exceptionally good. And if you're wondering why the Jones family selected a Steller's jay as their winery's mascot,

Jeanne explained: "It is a bird often seen in the foothills and the Sierra. When we were planning our first label, David and I thought it would be nice to have a bird and wanted one that was well known in the area."

Located just off of Hassler Road, Lava Cap is definitely not to be missed. As testament to their great product and very gracious, friendly, and knowledgeable staff, the tasting room is always busy. Inside you'll find a long tasting bar, and the winery's barrel room is visible through windows behind the bar. The Joneses encourage visitors to bring a picnic and enjoy some of the area's finest wines from the large deck, overlooking their vineyard. The winery also offers tours and group visits by appointment.

With 13 wines to choose from, visitors may pick five complimentary tastes. Lava Cap also has six Limited Reserve wines; reserve tasting is $5 per person, which can be applied toward a purchase.

FEATURED WINE: Petite Sirah
TASTING COST: Complimentary
HOURS: Daily, 11 AM–5 PM (except major holidays)
LOCATION: 2221 Fruitridge Road, Placerville
PHONE: 800-475-0175 or 530-621-0175
WEBSITE: www.lavacap.com

21 *Narrow Gate Vineyards*

Teena and Frank Hildebrand are passionate about life, and they share their passion with anyone who asks about their story. Prior to starting Narrow Gate Vineyards, the couple was living in Southern California. Involved for decades in the fashion industry, they were always passionate about wine; this passion turned into a desire to change their lifestyle and open a winery. In 2000, with faith strong in their hearts, they followed their calling and purchased 86 acres in southern Placerville that used to be a cattle ranch. With their own four hands, Teena and Frank planted their vineyard and built their gorgeous European-style winery.

"We are living our dream and keeping it fun and creative. Frank and I love people and want to encourage others to pursue their entrepreneurial dreams and help them overcome obstacles," said Teena. "We are a Christian married couple and include God in every phase of our operation. We openly talk about our faith when people ask and inspire others to pursue their dreams. Nothing is impossible with God."

Narrow Gate's name came straight out of the scriptures: Matthew 7:13–14 (New International Version), "Enter through the narrow gate . . . " Teena shared that when they were working toward their dream, there were many times that obstacles came up or doubts crossed her mind. Then she received a heaven-sent message that

Note the cross on the tasting room wall.

things would be okay while she and Frank were staking out a vineyard. Only Teena can tell the story about why an old branch, in the shape of a crucifix, hangs inside their tasting room above their entry door. If you enjoy stories about faith, be sure to ask her.

Frank is the winemaker, and Teena is the business manager and chef for their food and wine pairings. "I look forward to making and creating menus that really show off Frank's meticulous and specific wine-making style," Teena explained. A managerial economics major by way of the University of California at Davis, Frank has also worked through the university's winemaking extension courses. "He does everything by hand—no tanks, all barrel fermentation," said

Teena, noting that he uses traditional French wine-making techniques.

While the offerings at this small winery are wonderful, two are standouts. First is Dunamis, their best-selling red. A blend of Grenache, Syrah, and Mourvèdre, all of the grapes used are estate-grown. The other wine is their Chocolate Splash, a natural bittersweet chocolate-infused port. Made from six classic port varietals, the wine is infused with 60 percent dark bittersweet chocolate and 40 percent milk chocolate.

When entering their tasting room, visitors are bathed in romantic candlelight. The cellar doors, shutters, and tasting bar were once part of the property's old stable and bunkhouse, the latter of which housed ranch hands back in the 1940s. "A wind storm blew the roof off of both structures in 2002, so we used the wood in the winery's design," Teena explained. Also inside, artwork graces the tasting area, and the best part is that Teena or Frank, or both, will be there to pour you a taste. And on those gorgeous days, the Hildebrands invite you to enjoy their patio seating area where you can sip your wine and listen to the wind stir the pines above.

FEATURED WINES: Rhone blends
TASTING COST: Complimentary
HOURS: Friday and Saturday, 10 AM–5 PM; Sunday, 12 PM–5 PM
LOCATION: 4282 Pleasant Valley Road, Placerville
PHONE: 530-644-6201
WEBSITE: www.narrowgatevineyards.com

22 *Sierra Vista Vineyards and Winery*

Sierra Vista Vineyards and Winery has a view to outdo all other Sierra foothill wineries: Looking northeast from their picnic area, you'll see the magnificent Crystal Basin mountain range, part of Lake Tahoe's Desolation Wilderness. When the range is covered in snow, the view is even more breathtaking. Hence, the winery's name was a natural choice, made by winery owner and El Dorado County winemaking pioneer John Mac-Cready and his wife Barbara.

The MacCreadys found themselves just south of Placerville in the early 1970s because they were flat-out tired of moving: "As an engineer working for large companies, I was moved several times," said John, noting that besides being drained from moving all the time, they didn't want their children to become, as he put it, nomads. "We bought land in California and planted a vineyard. I commuted to Sacramento where I worked as a professor at California State University at Sacramento [electrical engineering], while we had a winery going. We have not had to move in 33 years." Their first crush took place in 1977, which coincided with the winery's opening. Today, Sierra Vista produces 7,000 cases of wine annually.

The MacCreadys pioneered the rebirth of "mountain viticulture." (To learn more about John Mac-Cready, read his winemaker interview at **www.Wine OhGuide.com.**) Sierra Vista's website, which is the

Sierra Vista's welcoming tasting room

most informative we saw while researching this book, talks about the topic. Extensive studies John conducted in the 1980s showed the climate at Sierra Vista to be very similar to that of the Northern Rhone Valley of France.

He used this information to determine which grape varieties to include in his vineyards. "High atop a curving ridge in the eastern highlands of California, our vineyards have wonderful soil for growing Rhone-style wine grapes. [The highlands] also have some of the best microclimates for different varieties . . . and one of the most spectacular views of any California wine region," John said. Today,

Sierra Vista's vineyard consists of 32 acres on slopes varying between 2800 and 2900 feet in elevation.

Sierra Vista's tagline is "The Northern Rhone Winery of El Dorado County," and they specialize in, what else, Rhone-style wines such as Syrah, Grenache, Mourvèdre, Viognier, and Roussanne. And with Rhone running deep in his Scottish blood, MacCready was the first president of the Rhone Rangers, a post he held for two years. A nationwide nonprofit with chapters in many regions, the organization is dedicated to promoting American Rhone varietal wines.

Champions of the environment, the MacCreadys installed photovoltaic solar panels at the winery in the late '90s; they were the first winery in the El Dorado viticulture area to do so. The 14.4-kilowatt system reduced energy consumption from the grid by about 94 percent the first month it was fully operational.

This eco-conscious winery also practices sustainable agriculture. The Sustainable Agriculture Research and Education Program at University of California at Davis (UC SAREP) emphasizes that "sustainable agriculture integrates three main goals—environmental health, economic profitability, and social and economic equity." The MacCreadys have implemented this philosophy into their daily agricultural practices and winery operations.

With all this said, the MacCreadys' hard work is evident by their success. And they enjoy working with each other day in and day out. As John explained, "I

WINE MYTH } The darker the color, the better the wine. No! A wine can be very dark in color but yet have very little fruit and aroma. It also may have a high alcohol content with residual sugar, which does not make a wine that goes well with food like wine should. **—John MacCready**

---

look forward to getting out of bed in the morning and saying, 'Hi, let's get to work,' and always having a glass of wine with her [my wife] in the evening after work."

Sierra Vista is on Cabernet Way at the end of Leisure Lane off Pleasant Valley Road, between Mt. Aukum and Newtown roads. The tasting room is charming, and the picnic grounds are canopied by large trees. According to MacCready, some wine lovers even visit in winter and picnic at the winery in short sleeves. To see the winery before going, check out their virtual tour offering on their website. They also host a blog (http://sierravistawinery.blogspot.com).

FEATURED WINES: Syrah, Viognier, and Fleur de Montagne, a Rhone-style blend
TASTING COST: Complimentary
HOURS: Daily, 11 AM–5 PM (except major holidays)
LOCATION: 4560 Cabernet Way, Placerville
PHONE: 800-WINE-916 or 530-622-7221
WEBSITE: www.sierravistawinery.com

SHINGLE SPRINGS

23 *Chevalier Winery*

Chevalier Winery, located in the serene French Creek Valley in southern Shingle Springs, makes true boutique wines with tenderness, humor, and a little "Swiss twist" thrown in. Owners Pierre and Jeanette Chevalier crushed their first harvest in 2001 and opened their winery in 2003 next to the site of California's first commercial winery, Watkins Ranch. The old vines from Watkins have grown up and into several stately oak trees on Chevalier property. "At that time (1852), French Creek Valley was inhabited by a bunch of French wine- and brandy-thirsty miners," Pierre said. A photo of the Watkins tending their vineyard is displayed in their tasting room, and Pierre shares his thoughts on "old vines that aren't cloned" in his fun winemaker interview, which you can read at **www.WineOhGuide.com.**

You can probably guess that the Swiss twist in this story is Pierre. Born and raised in Switzerland, Pierre came to the U.S. in the 1960s. He headed to the West Coast after he and his first wife divorced, and met Jeanette at a Presbyterian church in the Sacramento area. "They had a ministry for divorced people and

Courtesy of Chevalier Winery

Entrance to the Shingle Springs tasting room

that's how we met. It's been 15 years now," Pierre said
in his thick accent, glancing flirtatiously at his wife.

Jeanette grew up on the property. Her father purchased the land in 1943 (240 acres for only $1,800) and
moved his family here from Los Angeles in the 1950s
when Jeanette was 9 years old. She and her siblings at-
tended the one-room schoolhouse just down the road.

When Jeanette first brought Pierre to the ranch many years later, he liked everything except the weeds, especially the star thistle. Having been raised in Switzerland during World War II, where every square foot of arable land was cultivated, he couldn't stand the sight of weeds.

"We planted tomatoes to get rid of the thistles first. I wanted to plant grapes, because I figured I'm going to be retired some day, and what am I going to do?" he said, putting both hands in the air and playfully shrugging. The tomatoes grew like crazy but didn't produce fruit until that August, which was unusual. Later they learned that for tomatoes to set fruit, the temperature had to be between 55°F and 95°F; at the bottom of French Creek Valley, where the Chevaliers lived, the temperature dipped regularly into the 40s during the summer months. While this was bad news for tomato lovers, it was a revelation for Pierre and Jeanette—they knew their special microclimate was perfect for their Cabernet and Merlot grapes!

The boutique winery is definitely a passion, and it shows in their wines. According to Pierre, "We try to identify our winery with the making of fine wines to complement fine foods versus making 'boozy' wines for cocktails!" And that they do. One of their more prominent wines is called One Pearl. An estate Cabernet Sauvignon, the label used is a famous painting by Dutch painter Johannes Vermeer (1632–1675). Vermeer painted only 35 canvases, and the one featured on the label is his masterpiece *Girl with a Pearl Earring*. Referred to by art critics as the "Mona Lisa of the North," Vermeer and the model are probably best known in Tracy Chevalier's 2001 book named after the painting and the 2003 movie adaptation, starring Scarlett Johansson and Colin Firth. If you didn't catch the author's last name, look again: She is Pierre's cousin.

WINE MYTH } **Elevation makes better wines. —Pierre Chevalier**

The tasting room in Shingle Springs is down a hill behind the couple's home. When entering, you head by an old barn to the left, which has been there for more than a century. Arriving at the tasting room, be sure to look across the creek at the old oak trees; there you'll find those original 150-plus-year-old vines, hanging in the trees. And don't be surprised if their adorably friendly Australian shepherd, Queenie, meets you at your car and leads you into the tasting room.

The Chevaliers have a second tasting room on the corner of Pleasant Valley Road and Bucks Bar Road in Placerville.

FEATURED WINES: Cabernet and Merlot
TASTING COST: Complimentary
HOURS: Saturday and Sunday, 12 PM–5 PM (same for both locations)
LOCATION: *Main Tasting Room:* 5720 French Creek Road, Shingle Springs; *Secondary Tasting Room:* 2530 Pleasant Valley Road, Placerville
PHONE: 530-677-1676
WEBSITE: www.cabernetboutique.com

SOMERSET

24 *Busby Cellars*

Busby Cellars has been making great Zinfandels for a decade, and owners Elliott and Sherrie Graham do it all themselves. "We were looking for a fun and challenging profession that would allow us to be involved in every aspect of the business," said Sherrie, whose maiden name is Busby, hence the name of their winery. Per the Grahams, 100 percent of their wine is made on-site and they average 2,000 cases annually. "We do almost everything ourselves. From planting the vineyard to crushing, barreling, and bottling the wine, to running the tasting room, we really get our hands dirty!"

The Grahams wholeheartedly embrace the Zinfandel grape. "Why fight it?" Elliott asked. "The foothills are famous for world-class Zins—we might as well embrace California's noble grape!" Busby Cellars typically produces three to four different Zinfandels each year, all of which, according to Sherrie, "[offer] a unique translation of the varietal."

Elliott was introduced to winemaking by his father Larry Graham, an experienced home winemaker. "Larry enjoyed working with fruits such as plums and berries in addition to grapes, and Elliot was exposed to the fermentation and winemaking process at a very early age. After classes in viticulture and enology at the University of California at Davis, as well as experimenting with home winemaking himself, Elliot felt ready for the challenge of making wine on a larger scale," Sherrie explained. Since retiring in 2005, Larry helps out at the winery, much to his son's and daughter-in-law's delight.

Busby Cellars is located on a 34-acre portion of the historic Meyers Ranch; George D. H. Meyers, the namesake of the small Highway 50 town of Meyers near South Lake Tahoe, gave the property to his son George H. D. Meyers (same name, reversed middle initials) as a wedding present. D. H. purchased Yank's Station in the western South Lake Tahoe Basin (near the present-day California Agricultural Inspection Station) from Ephraim "Yank" Clement in 1873. He changed the name to Meyer's Station and operated the hotel and store until they both burnt down in 1938. Eventually the small town was simplified to Meyers.

Today, the historic 1930s Meyers Barn, one of two places where Grizzly Flat miners stopped to change horses on their way to Placerville, can be found in the Grahams' vineyard and is visible from the tasting room. The barn is used for equipment storage and recently served as a backdrop for a movie.

The winery's tasting room was built by Elliott with the help of friends and neighbors. Perched atop a small hill, the tasting room overlooks the Grahams' vine-

A selection of Busby Cellars's wines

yards and portions of the valley. The Grahams' official greeter is Hank the winery dog. A German shorthaired pointer, Hank welcomes customers in the parking lot and leads them to the tasting room door. Hank's photo has graced the pages of the celebrated *Wine Dog* series (www.winedogs.com).

FEATURED WINE: Zinfandel
TASTING COST: Complimentary
HOURS: Friday–Sunday, 11 AM–5:30 PM
LOCATION: 6375 Grizzly Flat Road, Somerset
PHONE: 530-344-9119
WEBSITE: www.busbycellars.com

25 *Cantiga Wineworks*

At Cantiga Wineworks, owners Christine and Rich Rorden do things differently. For instance, Cantiga is one of the only wineries in California to produce non-malolactic red wines. "Our winemaking style is as old as the hills," laughed Rich. And he may be right.

Normally, a wine goes through two fermentation processes. During the primary fermentation, yeast converts sugar to alcohol. During the second fermentation, also known as malolactic conversion, a strain of lactic bacteria converts the tart malic acid to a softer-tasting lactic acid. The latter fermentation sometimes occurs naturally, but most commercial winemakers initiate the process by inoculating the wine with bacteria, which deters undesirable bacterial strains from producing off-flavors. The main result is a wine that is less acidic, but one that also imparts a telling flavor change from what a grape would naturally create.

The Rordens have opted to prevent the secondary fermentation from occurring, noting that this age-old style of winemaking gives their wines crispness and pronounced fruit flavor for pairings with food, one of their passions. "Our goal is to make wine for the dinner table, which is more of an old-world idea," explained Christine. "Our non-malolactic method is one of the ways to achieve this—brighter acidity balances better with the acidity of most foods. Our wines tend to attract people who love to cook gourmet."

A self-taught winemaker, Rich is deeply rooted in winemaking tradition. "Rich is not swayed by contemporary trends," explained Christine. "Although modern enology has developed numerous methods for manipulating wine and achieving consistency, we have opted for minimal intervention . . . [we use] a gentle touch as winemakers to let the grapes—and the uniqueness of the vintage—speak for themselves."

One point that Christine brought up was both humorous and contemplative: Because their wines are very natural and pure, with extremely low sulfites, customers with wine allergies or sensitivities have reported to them that they do not experience headaches, stuffiness, or hangovers when they partake in Cantiga wine. "Although we are still researching the phenomenon and cannot legally make a claim to having 'hangover-free' wines, the customer testimonials are piling up!" she said.

A pivotal person in the Rorden family is Rich's father Bud, an accomplished amateur winemaker. The younger Rorden had been making wine beside his father since he was a little tot and always had an interest in the art form, so when he and Christine tired of the fast-paced life of Los Angeles—Rich was a mechanical engineer in the aerospace industry and Christine, an educational writer and ethnomusicologist (study of social and cultural aspects of music and dance in

A few of Cantiga's liquid offerings

local and global contexts)—the two felt that opening a commercial winery was a natural fit.

"We figured that if we were going to see the sun go down from our office windows every night, we might as well be working that hard for ourselves!" Christine confessed. The couple purchased 20 acres in Somerset, planted a little more than 5 acres in vineyards, and opened Cantiga Wineworks in 2000.

This small, multigenerational family winery is all hands-on, from the selection of fruit to the tasting room staffing. From Rich's and Christine's parents to their two young children (both under the age of six), everyone helps out. And their name is unique in the fact that it is a medieval Spanish song form. "We chose the name not only to honor the old European roots of our tradition, as well as the Spanish roots of winemaking in California, but also because I am an early music buff," said Christine, who can play the Renaissance lute. "Our label is an adaptation of a medieval woodblock print and is reminiscent of the illuminated manuscripts of the cantigas."

The Rorden's winery is reflective of medieval style, from its furnishings to its atmosphere. On a small knoll under towering pines, the winery is serene with an inviting adjacent patio, as well as gardens. The tasting room staff is friendly and knowledgeable, and they gently encourage you to relax and enjoy their wines, paired with their latest culinary creations.

FEATURED WINES: Non-malolactic Rhones, Zinfandel, and Chardonnay
TASTING COST: Free
HOURS: Friday–Sunday, 11 AM–5 PM
LOCATION: 5980 Meyers Lane, Somerset
PHONE: 530-621-1696
WEBSITE: www.cantigawine.com

26 *Windwalker Vineyard and Winery*

The evolution of Windwalker Vineyard and Winery from a vineyard to a successful winery required the dedication of many and the good fortune of a few. Originally, the gorgeous property and the vineyard planted in 1984 were named for the owner, L. W. Richard. In 1991, the Bailey family purchased the property and using their estate-grown grapes, opened Windwalker Vineyard and Winery. They named their new business after their stallion, because as legend has it, the "racing horse flew like the wind." A few years later, Arnie and Paige Gilpin bought the winery and brought it into the 21st century.

In the meantime, an amateur home winemaker from Placerville by the name of Jim Taff decided he wanted to take his craft to the next level. Having made wine on his own for more than 20 years, he volunteered at Windwalker, a stint that would last 13 years until he purchased the winery and its 20-plus acres from the Gilpins in 2007.

And as good fortune would have it, Taff married his longtime girlfriend Alanna on the winery's 2,000-square-foot redwood deck in 1995, six years before he bought the winery. "It's wild to think that we got married on the deck," said Taff, "then we ended up owning the place." Their two-story Tudor-style home is adjacent to the winery and its sizeable deck, shaded by a massive oak that comes up through the flooring.

Windwalker's tasting room and gift boutique

With 9.5 acres of vineyard planted, the winery today produces 10,000 cases a year. Their winemaker is Dominic Mantei, who, as Alanna shared, is a "very worthy young man who lives on the property and we are very proud of him!" Their flagship wine is a 2006 Barbera Cooper Vineyard made with grapes from the Dick Cooper Ranch in Amador County (see page 188). According to Taff, in 2000 they entered their 1997 Barbera into a wine competition and won for best red wine in California (under $20). "We've never competed again after that win," said Taff, remarking that all of their ribbons and awards are tucked away in a box somewhere.

But the Taffs don't need tons of ribbons and awards to decorate their tasting room; their wine is so good that it's not uncommon for wine lovers to be three deep at the bar. Their tasting room is easily one of the biggest in El Dorado County, with its soaring open-ceiling construction, skylights, and beautiful tiled floors. Their gift boutique makes you feel you're at a high-end home decor store, and they also offer gourmet food items, kitchenware, and wine accessories. The facility also has a 1,000-square-foot party room with a full commercial kitchen, perfect for weddings, special events, and anniversary and birthday parties.

Outside you'll find the large redwood deck with seating areas, as well as two additional picnic areas overlooking the vineyards and a large seasonal pond. And if you happen upon a border collie/Australian shepherd mix named Wino, then you've met the Taffs' official greeter. Wino was recently featured in the celebrated *Wine Dog* series (www.winedogs.com), so he's used to the attention!

FEATURED WINES: Grand Chardonnay, Barbera, Zinfandel, and Ruby Port
TASTING COST: Complimentary
HOURS: Daily, 11 AM–5 PM
LOCATION: 7360 Perry Creek Road, Somerset
PHONE: 530-620-4054
WEBSITE: www.windwalkervineyard.com

+ More Area Wineries

CAMINO

Auriga Wine Cellars
HOURS: Friday–Sunday, 11 AM–5 PM
LOCATION: 3500 Carson Road, Building D, Camino
PHONE: 530-647-8078
WEBSITE: www.aurigawines.com

Garnet Sun Winery
HOURS: Check website for hours
LOCATION: 3500 Carson Road, Building C, Camino
PHONE: 530-647-VINO (8466)
WEBSITE: www.garnetsun.com

Illuminare Estate
HOURS: Friday–Sunday, 11 AM–5 PM
LOCATION: 3500 Carson Road, Building B, Camino
PHONE: 530 306-3873
WEBSITE: www.illuminarewinery.com

ParaVi Vineyards
HOURS: Daily (except Tuesday), 11 AM–5 PM
LOCATION: 2875 Larsen Drive, Camino
PHONE: 530-647-9463
WEBSITE: www.paravivineyards.com

Stone's Throw Winery
HOURS: Call for hours
LOCATION: 3541 North Canyon Road, Camino
PHONE: 530-622-5100
WEBSITE: None available

Ursa Vineyards
HOURS: Friday, 1 PM–5 PM; Saturday and Sunday, 11 AM–5 PM
LOCATION: 3550 Carson Road, Camino
PHONE: 530-647-2646
WEBSITE: www.ursavineyards.com

FAIR PLAY

Barkley Historic Homestead Winery
HOURS: Saturday and Sunday, 11 AM–5 PM
LOCATION: 8320 Stoney Creek Road, Fair Play
PHONE: 888-708-4466 or 530-620-6783
WEBSITE: www.barkleyhomestead.com

Fitzpatrick Winery and Lodge
HOURS: Wednesday–Monday, 11 AM–5 PM
LOCATION: 7740 Fair Play Road, Fair Play
PHONE: 800-245-9166
WEBSITE: www.fitzpatrickwinery.com

MV Winery – Miller Vineyards
HOURS: Wednesday–Sunday, 11 AM–5 PM
LOCATION: 7261 Fair Play Road, Fair Play
PHONE: 530-620-1067
WEBSITE: None listed

Oakstone Winery
HOURS: Wednesday–Sunday, 11 AM–5 PM
LOCATION: 6440 Slug Gulch Road, Fair Play
PHONE: 530-620-5303
WEBSITE: www.oakstone-winery.com

Single Leaf Vineyards and Winery
HOURS: Wednesday–Sunday, 11 AM–5 PM
LOCATION: 7480 Fair Play Road, Fair Play
PHONE: 530-620-5818
WEBSITE: www.singleleaf.com

Van der Vijver Estate Winery
HOURS: Check website
LOCATION: 2800 Omo Ranch Road, Fair Play
PHONE: 530-620-5818
WEBSITE: www.zinwithus.com

Winery by the Creek
HOURS: Thursday–Sunday, 11 AM–5 PM
LOCATION: 7451 Fair Play Road, Fair Play
PHONE: 530-620-3210
WEBSITE: www.winerybythecreek.com

MOUNT AUKUM

Chateau Routon
HOURS: Wednesday–Sunday, 11 AM–5 PM
LOCATION: 2800 Omo Ranch Road, Mt. Aukum
PHONE: 530-620-5818
WEBSITE: www.chateauroutoninc.com

Mount Aukum Winery
HOURS: Daily, 11 AM–5 PM
LOCATION: 6781 Tower Road, Mt. Aukum
PHONE: 800-591-9463
WEBSITE: www.mountaukum.com

PILOT HILL

Venezio Vineyards and Winery
HOURS: Wednesday–Sunday, 11 AM–5 PM
LOCATION: 5821 Highway 49, Pilot Hill
PHONE: 530-885-WINE (9463)
WEBSITE: www.venezio.com

PLACERVILLE

Boa Vista Orchards
HOURS: Daily, 8:30 AM–5:30 PM
LOCATION: 2952 Carson Road, Placerville
PHONE: 866-MtGrown (684-7696) or 530-622-5522
WEBSITE: www.boavista.com

Gold Hill Vineyard
HOURS: Thursday–Sunday, 10 AM–5 PM
LOCATION: 5660 Vineyard Lane, Placerville
PHONE: 530-626-6522
WEBSITE: www.goldhillvineyard.com

Miraflores Winery
HOURS: Daily, 10 AM–5 PM
LOCATION: 2120 Four Springs Trail, Placerville
PHONE: 530-647-8505
WEBSITE: www.mirafloreswinery.com

SHINGLE SPRINGS

Sogno Winery
HOURS: Check website
LOCATION: 3046 Ponderosa Road, Shingle Springs
PHONE: 530-672-6968
WEBSITE: www.sognowinery.com

SIDE TRIPS

Highway 50 passes through the heart of **Placerville** (www.cityofplacerville.org). The county seat, Placerville has a wonderful downtown district coined the **Downtown Main Street** (www.placerville-downtown.org). Here you'll find old buildings galore, now filled with assorted restaurants and shops. But history still lurks, and during your visit, you'll probably see lots of references to **"Hangtown,"** one of Placerville's original names.

The story goes that in 1849, a gambler by the name of Lopez won big at the local saloon. When he decided to retire for the evening, several upset men tried to steal his winnings. Lopez fought back, and with the help of others, overpowered the robbers. It was determined that three of the robbers were wanted for murder, so after a short 30-minute trial, they were found guilty and the crowd demanded they be hanged. The tree for the evil-doing was in Elstner's Hay Yard, next to the Jackass Inn. Today, the stump from this infamous tree can be found in the cellar of the Hangman's Tree Tavern.

Another important historic Main Street landmark is the **Bell Tower.** A monument to the city's volunteer firemen, the 1865 tower came about after three major fires wiped out Placerville's business section. The cost to construct the tower was $380. Today, the tower is the focal point for the city's celebrations.

Nearby, Placerville's **Gold Bug Park and Mine** (www.goldbugpark.org) features a real gold mine that began in 1888 and today is open for tours. Although it is no longer a working mine, on the tours you can try your hand at banging a single jackhammer as the old miners did when "drilling" holes for dynamite charges—110 feet below the surface. There is also another mine in the park, the **Priest Mine,** that can be seen only on guided tours. Plus, there's a stamp mill (where ore was crushed) and a gift shop. And if you're feeling the fever, you can rent a gold pan and do a little gold mining yourself.

Eight miles north of Placerville, on Highway 49, is the site of gold discovery. In January 1848 while checking the millstream of John Sutter's **Coloma** sawmill, James Marshall discovered several gold nuggets. When word got out, gold fever enveloped the entire world, triggering one of the largest and fastest human migrations in world history. California's Gold Rush and the discovery of gold are celebrated at **Marshall Gold Discovery State Historic Park** (www.parks.ca.gov). In addition to a museum, a historic Chinese drugstore, and several reconstructed buildings, the famed sawmill has been reconstructed and rangers periodically demonstrate how it works. A short walk up a steep hill, or a short drive around the back side, will take you to the Marshall monument where James Marshall is buried. There is also a historic cemetery not far away.

SIDE TRIPS

SIDE TRIPS

About 10 miles east of Placerville is the town of **Camino,** home of the ever-so-popular tourist area known as **Apple Hill** (www.applehill.com). Each year, tens of thousands of people come here to buy pumpkins for Halloween, as well as apple pies, apple donuts, apple crisp, caramel apples, apple fritters, apple turnovers, and, believe it or not, plain old apples. You can watch apples being squished into cider or wander though hundreds of craft booths scattered among the dozens of different destinations throughout the region. This is a great place for kids to run in the country—and eat apples plucked right from a tree.

A few miles west of Placerville, just off on Highway 50 and adjacent to the El Dorado County Fairgrounds, you'll find the **El Dorado County Historical Museum** (www.co.el-dorado.ca.us/museum), one of the best county museums in the Sierra foothills. The staff takes great care in presenting the museum's artifacts and showcasing their place in history. Here you'll find exhibits and artifacts on the Pony Express, area gold panning and logging, a wheelbarrow made locally by a very young John Studebaker (before his automobile days), and even a pair of 9-foot-long, 25-pound skis that the famous John "Snowshoe" Thompson used to deliver mail over the Sierra Nevada for 20 years.

For More Information

El Dorado Winery Association
P.O. Box 1614
Placerville, CA 95667
800-306-3956
www.eldoradowines.org

Fair Play Winery Association
P.O. Box 341
Fair Play, CA 95684
www.fairplaywine.com

El Dorado County Visitors Authority
c/o Chamber of Commerce
542 Main Street
Placerville, CA 95667
800-457-6279 or 530-621-5885
www.visit-eldorado.com

Carson Road Wineries Association
3550 Carson Road
Camino, CA 95709
530-647-1767

Apple Hill Growers Association
P.O. Box 494
Camino, CA 95709
530-644-7692
www.applehill.com

El Dorado County Farm Trails Association
3987 Missouri Flat Road
Placerville, CA 95667
www.edc-farmtrails.org

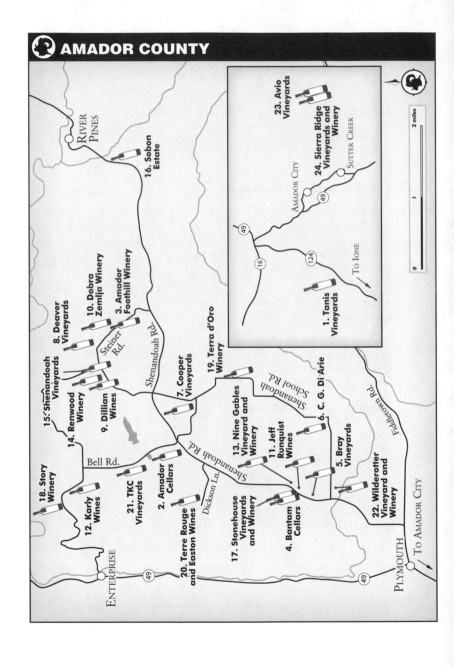

AMADOR COUNTY

RIVER PINES

16. Sobon Estate

23. Avio Vineyards

24. Sierra Ridge Vineyards and Winery

SUTTER CREEK

AMADOR CITY

49

124

To Ione

1. Tanis Vineyards

16

49

2 miles

0   1

8. Deaver Vineyards

10. Dobra Zemlja Winery

3. Amador Foothill Winery

Steiner Rd.

Shenandoah Rd.

19. Terra d'Oro Winery

15. Shenandoah Vineyards

14. Renwood Winery

9. Dillian Wines

7. Cooper Vineyards

Shenandoah School Rd.

6. C. G. Di Arie

13. Nine Gables Vineyard and Winery

11. Jeff Runquist Wines

5. Bray Vineyards

18. Story Winery

Bell Rd.

21. TKC Vineyards

2. Amador Cellars

Dickson Ln.

Shenandoah Rd.

17. Stonehouse Vineyards and Winery

4. Bantam Cellars

22. Wilderotter Vineyard and Winery

Fiddletown Rd.

12. Karly Wines

ENTERPRISE

49

20. Terre Rouge and Easton Wines

PLYMOUTH

49

To Amador City

Sierra
Foothills

4

★ Amador County

Gold put Amador County on the map as mining town after mining town sprang up faster than spring wildflowers, and most of the tent-towns died just as fast as the gold quickly played out and the miners moved on. What a few of those more knowledgeable and thirsty miners discovered was that the foothills had the perfect climate and great soils for growing grapes, especially Zinfandel grapes. And since most of those thousands of miners were in constant need of alcohol, wine seemed to be a more valuable commodity than gold—at least it was much easier to produce.

Amador County has the distinction of being the only county in the state named after a native Californian. While the region was still under Mexican control, Jose Maria Amador had become a wealthy landowner. In 1848 and 1849, Amador took several of his employees across the valley to the Sierra foothills to mine for gold. The creek they mined and the mining settlements that followed became known as Amadore's Creek,

Amadore Crossing, and Amadore City. In 1854 when parts of the original Calaveras County were sliced off to create some new, smaller counties, the name Amador was selected for this new California county.

With Amador County's elevations ranging from 200 feet above sea level to 9000 feet, there is much to do here—and much of the activity focuses on the great outdoors. While Highway 88 offers great hiking and fishing opportunities galore, and even prominent ski areas such as Kirkwood Ski Resort, Highway 49 passes through numerous surviving Gold Rush towns. Some of those towns, such as Jackson, had long-lived gold mining operations. Following the placer gold's easy pickin's, someone discovered gold lodged in quartz rock that was scattered all about. The age of hard-rock mining had begun. Operations like Jackson's Kennedy Mine, discovered in 1860, ran continuously to 1942. One of the deepest mines in the world, it produced more than $32 million—when gold prices were controlled by U.S. law and the price never went above $35 per ounce.

Long before the gold miners arrived, the Miwok lived throughout this area of the Sierra foothills. Mortars worn into large chunks of granite, often near streams, are a testament to their ability to survive here for thousands of years. Expansive oak woodlands provided acorns, wild bulbs, and wildlife as steady sources of food. Their history remains alive at Indian Grinding Rock State Historic Park, east of Jackson.

The wine industry got off to a slow start in Amador County. It is believed that Swiss immigrant Adam Uhlinger founded the first winery in the county—and one of the first commercial wineries in California—in 1856. He is also believed to be the first to have planted Zinfandel grapes, a mainstay of most Sierra foothill wineries today. During 13 years of Prohibition, the winery had to resort to making only small quantities of wine that could be sold to churches and to selling table grapes to stay in business. That same winery—Sobon Estate, now owned by Leon and Shirley Sobon—has a great wincry museum in the original winery building.

Today, more than 30 wineries and hundreds of acres of vineyards dot these Sierra foothills that once were the home of the Miwok. As you drive the backroads through towns with Gold Rush–era names such as Fiddletown, Drytown, Sutter Creek, and Mount Aukum, remember that in Amador County you are surrounded by an exciting history—one that goes back thousands of years.

IONE

1 *Tanis Vineyards*

Tanis Vineyards, located in northern Ione a few miles south of Highway 16, is one of Amador County's up-and-coming wineries. Established in January 2008, the winery is the result of Andrew Tanis's "hobby gone wild," according to his wife Jill, who noted that winemaking has been Andrew's passion and dream for many years. Before they moved to Ione, the couple and their two young children lived in Elk Grove, south of Sacramento. Andrew released his first wine in 2005 and hasn't looked back. The small size of his winery has not hindered him from creating a dozen offerings with an emphasis on Italian varietals.

When they purchased their 2 acres, it was covered in poison oak. Slowly, the Tanises eradicated the menace and planted their vineyard, only to be challenged by Mother Nature again at harvest time; while hand-pressing grapes in the vineyard, Andrew's wedding ring slipped from his finger, sinking into the rich soil that he had worked so hard to nurture. Try as they may, they never found the ring.

If you look closely at the Tanis wine label, you'll see their story. There's that dreaded poison oak on one side

A selection of Tanis Vineyards's wines

of the label and healthy grapes and vines on the other. In the middle is the missing wedding band with the inscription "faith, love, and hope" in Italian. Through the many challenges encountered while following their dream, it's apparent that the Tanises see the wine glass as half full, not half empty.

The tasting room, which is adjacent to their home, is small and inviting and features many gourmet food items under their label. Talking with Andrew, you quickly realize he is passionate about his craft (to learn more about Andrew, read his winemaker interview at **www.WineOhGuide.com**). One fun story has to do with their popular TNT label and, appropriately, their

blend called Dynamite Red. The name came about because it took more than muscle to remove the Volk-
swagen-sized boulders from their Zinfandel vineyard.
Where there's a will, there's a way, and nothing will
deter Andrew and Jill Tanis from becoming another
popular winery in Amador County!

FEATURED WINES: Primitivo, Syrah, Cabernet Franc, and Petite Sirah
TASTING COST: Complimentary
HOURS: Saturday and Sunday, 10 AM–5:30 PM
LOCATION: 13120 Willow Creek Road, Ione
PHONE: 209-274-4807
WEBSITE: www.tanisvineyards.com

PLYMOUTH

2 Amador Cellars

Amador Cellars is a treat to visit. Found just off Shenandoah Road, the winery is nestled beneath a stand of
very large valley oaks. Winery dogs Bailey and Kali are
the official greeters, and the shaded patio area is inviting. Inside, you'll more than likely be poured a yummy
taste by a member of the Long family.

"Family always makes for an enjoyable and easy time,"
said co-owner/winemaker Larry Long when asked about

working with relatives. The tasting room crew includes co-owner/wife Linda, daughter Ashley, son Michael, 85-year-old father Bill (called "Pops" by everyone), sister Linda, and nephew Brian. "Our family-staffed winery provides guests with a friendly and fun wine-tasting experience," he said, adding that even more of the Long gang and friends help out during special winery events.

A farmer and winemaker since 1990, Long makes his wares on the premises. The tasting room shares its space with the actual winery, so while you enjoy Long's wares, you can also view huge stainless steel tanks and lots of barrels. As their brochure explains: "Our wines are made in a style that emphasizes varietal character of the fruit augmented by subtle oak and vanilla flavors from oak-barrel aging." Immediately outside the door are acres upon acres of grapevines, and if you're lucky enough to be there in the evening, you'll be treated to a beautiful sunset over the vineyards.

Amador Cellars is one of the environmentally-friendly leaders in Amador County when it comes to winery construction. Built in 2003, the winery is made of rice straw bales and concrete; its two-foot-thick tall walls tower over the tasting room. You can check out the construction for yourself on their website—there you'll find photos and a detailed explanation of the building process, right down to insulation ratings and truss construction

When asked about the name of their winery, Long explained: "Amador County needed an 'Amador Cellars

Amador Cellars's tasting room and winery

Winery'—we wanted to keep it nice and simple." And that they have, from their winery with its beautiful old-world construction and style to their exquisite wine selections to their fun family atmosphere. Without a doubt, this winery should make its namesake proud.

FEATURED WINE: Zinfandel
TASTING COST: Complimentary
HOURS: Monday–Friday, 12 PM–5 PM; Saturday and Sunday, 11 AM–5 PM
LOCATION: 11093 Shenandoah Road, Plymouth
PHONE: 209-245-6150
WEBSITE: www.amadorcellars.com

3 *Amador Foothill Winery*

Finding a better way to do things is commonplace at Amador Foothill Winery, as co-owner Ben Zeitman and his wife, co-owner and winemaker Katie Quinn, have always done things a little differently. Perched atop a hill where the 1700-foot elevation offers a bird's-eye view of the goings on along Steiner Road and beyond, the winery is a hobby gone out of control for Zeitman. Opening in 1980, and with the expertise of Quinn, who holds a master's degree in enology from the University of California at Davis, the couple has been forging new paths when it comes to the industry and art of winemaking.

WINE MYTH } More money always gets you a better bottle.
—Ben Zeitman

Wanting to make a difference in the world, Zeitman and Quinn have been involved with the national Communicating for America Education Programs (CAEP). This nonprofit membership organization offers scholarships, educational training, and exchange and hosting opportunities for students from all over the world in a variety of agricultural-related programs.

For more than a decade, the winery has hosted enology students during harvest time to work the fields and help make the wine. They have hosted people from all parts of the globe, but according to Zeitman, the last few

The view from the winery

years the exchange students have been from Italy. "We know a very famous winemaker in Italy who finds people for us and they come to us through this program," explained Zeitman, citing that most have some type of agricultural degree. The couple boards the students in their home, and the students are eager learners, grateful for the opportunity to come to the U.S. to work a harvest.

With regard to the environment, Amador Foothill has reduced their carbon footprint by using an energy-efficient rock bed cooling system for their wine cellar. A passive cooling system encompassing two levels and built into a north-facing hillside, the rock bed itself is 8 feet high, 3 feet wide, and 50 feet long. The rocks are about 8 inches in diameter and are placed with enough

Amador Foothill's tasting room and winery

open space in-between for air to easily pass through;
using no electrical fans or electrical source of any kind,
the outside air comes inside through three different areas in the lower cellar, forcing the hot air out through
ceiling vents. As far as Zeitman knows, no other winery is using this earth-friendly cooling system. You can
see a part of this system through a large window in the
tasting room, overlooking the wine cellar.

FEATURED WINES: Zinfandel, Sangiovese, and a Rhone blend
TASTING COST: Complimentary
HOURS: Friday–Sunday, 12 PM–5 PM
LOCATION: 12500 Steiner Road, Plymouth
PHONE: 800-778-WINE (9463) or 209-245-6307
WEBSITE: www.amadorfoothill.com

4 *Bantam Cellars*

Throughout your wine travels, you've probably noticed varying styles of tasting rooms, from classic to modern, down-home to uptown, even outdoorsy to "cavey" (if there is such a word). But at Bantam Cellars, the style is "barn-chic," chickens and all.

This winery resembles an upscale barn; the inside is classy with its tongue-in-groove knotty pine and a crystal chandelier lighting the four-sided tasting bar. Their wine is served in stemless glasses, and they offer free walnuts. The winery's gift shop features hens and roosters, of course! Bantam's name is apropos considering co-owner Jonna Cobb loves everything capon: She's raised bantam hens and roosters her entire life. If you're lucky, you might even be able to feed a few of the "winery chickens" at the door.

WINE MYTH } "Real" corks are better than synthetic corks.
        —Jonna Cobb

Jonna's husband Garth is the son of Amador County winemaking icons Buck and Karly Cobb (Karly Wines, see page 200). Garth, who is also a co-owner of the winery, is the youngest of his siblings and started making wines with his father in the late 1970s. According to Jonna, "He is frequently asked if he went to school to learn to make wine; his answer usually is 'not enough to

Bantam Cellars's "barn-chic" tasting room

screw up my winemaking.' He and Buck take extension courses through Davis every now and again, but most of the wine education has been a hands-on experience."

Bantam opened in 2007, and most of its wines are made at "big sister" Karly. As Cobb explained, "We're excited to open a tasting room on the main road . . . we've been off the beaten path at Karly for nearly 30 years. We also wanted to experiment with our passion for true Italian varietals, while at Karly we concentrate on more Mediterranean varietals."

Besides being a co-owner, general manager, and a chef, Jonna oversees their wine club, the "Peeps."

She also hosts a fun "party blog" in which she shares their winery's current doings, and posts recipes as well (www.jonnag.wordpress.com).

FEATURED WINES: Barbera, Sangiovese, Primitivo, and Vermentino
TASTING COST: Complimentary
HOURS: Daily, 11 AM–4 PM
LOCATION: 10851 Shenandoah Road, Plymouth
PHONE: 209-245-6677
WEBSITE: www.bantamcellars.com

---

5 Bray Vineyards

One of the first destinations on the way into the Amador County wine region on Shenandoah Road is Bray Vineyards. From the outside, you may think that it simply looks like a nice winery, but once you step into their eclectic tasting room, you're in for one heck of a good time.

Yes, a good time, and that's just not evident by the name of one of the winery's most popular labels—Brayzin Hussy. Hanging over the tasting room bar is Ms. Hussy herself, an almost life-sized, red-haired doll sitting on a grapevine swing, decked out in little else but black stockings and a Zinfandel-red corset. A play on words using the winery's name, Brayzin Hussy is noted on its label as having "a bountiful body" and as being "excellent with

Stephanie Anderson and the Bray gang at play!

pizza, pasta, ribs, and most breakfast cereals." And don't be fooled by the red claw-foot bathtub outside; rest assured that is not where they make this wine! Robin and Oliver Bray's winery exudes high quality wines in both their products and presentation. They started in 1996, bottled their first wine in 2002, and opened their tasting room two years later. With more than 30 acres planted with 15 grape varietals, the vineyards are quite colorful, especially during the fall.

WINE MYTH } Mylar tape is tied to the vines to make sparkling wines! —*John Hoddy*

Things are quite colorful inside the tasting room, too, where you'll find staff decked out in either black or bright yellow Bray T-shirts. Items for sale include Bray-themed attire and their award-winning olive oil, made from their orchard. They offer freebies, too, from Bray and Brayzin Hussy buttons to key chains made from their leftover corks. And the winery's popularity is such that it's not uncommon to have customers several deep and upward of a half-dozen staff pouring at one time. But don't dismay; tasting wine at Bray is an experience, and a fun one at that. The atmosphere is festive and the playful banter between patrons and staff is contagious.

If you're real lucky, winemaker John Hoddy might jump on the pouring line when things get crazy. While at first glance he may appear conservative, he's quite the opposite; be sure to ask him about the Mylar tape found in the vineyards. He'll tell you a great story! To learn more about Hoddy, read his winemaker interview at **www.WineOhGuide.com**. And more than likely, Stephanie Anderson will be pouring; the winery's "jack-of-all-trades" with her infectious smile, kind spirit, and sense of humor will ensure you have a great time enjoying a great wine!

FEATURED WINES: Barbera, Petite Sirah, Sangiovese, and Verdelho
TASTING COST: Complimentary
HOURS: Friday–Monday, 10 AM–5 PM
LOCATION: 10590 Shenandoah Road, Plymouth
PHONE: 209-245-6023
WEBSITE: www.brayvineyards.com

---

6 C. G. Di Arie

For a truly unique and flavorful tasting experience, a stop at C. G. Di Arie winery is a must. The depth of the winery's offerings is phenomenal, and they are spiced with just enough boldness and exquisite flavor to garner the establishment award after major award.

The winery's name is unique. When trying to come up with a moniker for his newest venture and lifelong dream, winemaker and co-owner Chaim (pronounced hime) Gur-Arieh (the "h" is silent) decided to base it on his name. There are his initials (C and G) at the

Courtesy of C. G. Di Arie

Chaim Gur-Arieh

beginning, followed by "Di" (Gur-Arieh says he threw that in), followed by the phonetic part of his last name. While the name might be confusing for some, his wines are not.

The food industry—and namely flavors—is what Gur-Arieh is known for around the world. For his full story, read his winemaker interview at **www.WineOh Guide.com.** Here's a summary: In the early 1960s, while working at Quaker Oats, he developed the technology behind a very popular kid's breakfast cereal; he then developed puddings-in-a-cup and shelf-stable yogurts for Del Monte; soon after, he founded a major food development corporation where he created new products such as wine coolers, Power Bars, and the liquid version of Hidden Valley Ranch Dressing. In addition to all that, he founded a major flavor company that created a database of more than 5,000 flavors for the food industry.

After 25 years of running the flavoring company, Gur-Arieh and his wife Elisheva sold the business and purchased more than 200 acres in nearby El Dorado County. There they planted 40 acres of vineyards and built their world-class, gravity-fed winery. "I've developed a style of wine that is rather unique. My wines are fully extracted with fruit forward, good mid-palate and long finish, but, at the same time, they are elegant," Gur-Arieh explained in true winemaker lingo. He released his first wine in 2001. When asked what a visitor should not miss, Gur-Arieh declared, "Tasting at least one of my Gallery Collection Club wines."

Their wines are poured at their Plymouth tasting room. Outside, this charming winery features a stately deck overlooking a picnic area that gently slopes down to a koi pond, complete with a gurgling waterfall. Inside, you'll find a fine collection of art and wine. Elisheva has several original paintings on display and for sale.

WINE MYTH } Corks help the wine age better.
            —Chaim Gur-Arieh

"My wife does the art and I do the wine," Gur-Arieh said, flashing one of his famous grins from underneath his signature Australian cowboy hat.

FEATURED WINE: Zinfandel
TASTING COST: Complimentary
HOURS: Thursday–Monday, 10 AM–4:30 PM
LOCATION: 19919 Shenandoah School Road, Plymouth
PHONE: 209-245-4700
WEBSITE: www.cgdiarie.com

---

7 *Cooper Vineyards*

To make fine wines, you must have fine grapes. And the surname Cooper is synonymous with fine grapes, as the family has provided them to wineries for more than 30 years. Five generations of Coopers have farmed the lush Shenandoah Valley, with iconic grape grower Dick Cooper working the land himself for three decades. Cooper is known as the go-to guy by vintners all over the region who have questions or need help; he humbly and unselfishly gives of his time and lends his expertise, expecting nothing in return.

It wasn't until 2000 that Cooper, at the urging of his daughters, saved some of his crop and made his own wine. Because he had no winery facilities, the grapes were custom crushed by another business then bottled

Tasting room and winery at Cooper Vineyards

under the Cooper label. The wine turned out so well
that Cooper founded his own winery in December
2004. Two of his adult daughters, Jeri Swift and Chris-
ty Cooper Cheetham, oversee winery operations, but
Cooper stays out of their way. True to his roots and his
160 acres, he continues the legacy of providing quality
grapes to customers. (To learn more about Cooper, see
his interview at **www.WineOhGuide.com.**)

Cooper's Mediterranean-style tasting room sits
atop a small knoll overlooking the vineyards. The building doubles as the winery and is a great place to enjoy
your vino and relax underneath their large vine-draped
patio. One unusual decoration is the red 30/50 Twin

Indian motorcycle parked on a loft. According to Cooper, the motorcycle was a gift from good friend and fellow grape grower Jim Fox. "His place was two ranches down. We were such good neighbors and friends that we had breakfast together every morning in Plymouth," Cooper explained. Fox gave Cooper the motorcycle, which had been sitting in his garage, to display in his tasting room when construction was completed, but Fox was ill and passed away before the winery opened. The motorcycle's place of honor in the winery is a fitting tribute to Cooper's colleague and friend.

For you wine club lovers, listen up! Cooper's club is called "Cin Cin!" According to the winery's website: "It's been said that toasting turns the simple act of drinking wine into a ceremony. In Italy, *cin cin* (pronounced CHIN chin) is believed to recreate the sound of glasses touching during ceremonies of hospitality and friendship." Besides their very active wine club, the vineyard also hosts a blog (www.cooperwines.typepad.com).

FEATURED WINE: Barbera
TASTING COST: Complimentary
HOURS: Thursday–Monday, 11 AM–4:45 PM
LOCATION: 21365 Shenandoah School Road, Plymouth
PHONE: 209-245-6181
WEBSITE: www.cooperwines.com

8 *Deaver Vineyards*

Deaver Vineyards, on Steiner Road, has one of the region's deepest agricultural histories and is home to the Shenandoah Valley's oldest farming families. John A. Davis was one of the valley's first settlers, arriving in the 1850s from Iowa at the age of 22, according to Eric J. Costa, the author of *Old Vines: A History of Winegrowing in Amador County*. Costa, who is also the winemaker at Sierra Ridge Vineyards and Winery (see page 234), notes that Davis was a trained cooper (one who makes or repairs barrels or vats) and after having some luck in the gold fields, he turned to farming, establishing one of the region's finest fruit farms. Out of Davis's 117 acres, initially two were dedicated to vineyards, and by 1880, he was selling upward of 11,000 pounds of grapes annually. Davis found gold in his fruit ranching and worked the land until his death in 1910 at the age of 85.

WINE MYTH } **You need to drink specific wines while eating specific foods. —Ken Deaver**

More than 150 years and four generations later, Davis's great-grandson Ken Deaver takes care of the family's land, which stands at 300 acres. Of that acreage, eight are devoted to Mission vines, planted around 1853 by Davis, and Zinfandel vines planted by Deaver's grandfather Joseph Davis four decades later. But the

Deaver Vineyards's tasting room

Deaver family didn't start making wines for commercial purposes until the 1980s, when their first vintage Zinfandel was bottled under the Lakeshore label.

The family opened their tasting room in the late '80s, soon after the release of their first wine. Their place is picture-perfect: Their neatly manicured lawns, expansive picnic area, and beautiful oak-lined, tranquil lake speak to the family's pride, as does their charming, very large, and well-appointed barn-style tasting room, complete with boutique shopping opportunities. If you like shopping, the plethora of high-quality wares found at Deaver will make you giddy with delight!

Deaver is known worldwide for their Zinfandels, but their ports are just as popular. If you like to cook, check out the dozens of mouth-watering recipes on Deaver's website, all designed to be paired with their amazing wines, of course! And if you can't pull yourself away from the tasting bar, consider spending the weekend at the Amador Harvest Inn, the vineyard's bed-and-breakfast; once all the hustle and bustle of the wine traffic subsides, you have the place to yourself, and it is heavenly (www.amadorharvestinn.com).

FEATURED WINES: Zinfandel and ports
TASTING COST: Complimentary
HOURS: Daily, 10:30 AM–5 PM
LOCATION: 12455 Steiner Road, Plymouth
PHONE: 209-245-4099
WEBSITE: www.deavervineyard.com

9 *Dillian Wines*

The Dillian family opened its "home" to wine patrons in 2003. Tom Dillian's former home, and the site where his great-grandfather Alessio Dal Porto homesteaded back in 1917, this rich piece of land has been in the family ever since.

Owner Tom Dillian is also the winemaker and grape grower. When asked what makes his winery special, he said, "[We're a] father-and-son team specializing in regional varieties produced in limited quantities,"

Wine cork wreath at Dillian's tasting room entrance

referring to himself and his son Thomas, the fifth generation of Dillian men to work this land.

The tasting room is inviting from the outside, especially with the many seating areas found under the large wraparound porch. Inside, the mauve color of the tasting room bar is the highlight, drawing customers in to taste Dillian's offerings. And if you love old-fashioned gardens, an outside stroll with a glass of wine is a must.

FEATURED WINES: Barbera, Zinfandel, and Primitivo
TASTING COST: Complimentary
HOURS: Friday–Sunday, 11 AM–4:30 PM
LOCATION: 12138 Steiner Road, Plymouth
PHONE: 209-245-3444
WEBSITE: www.dillianwines.com

---

10 *Dobra Zemlja Winery*

A long, one lane driveway leads from Steiner Road across a tiny seasonal creek and up over a hill to Dobra Zemlja Winery. After parking next to the winery's small lake, don't be surprised if a guy sporting a long, white, bushy mustache, shaggy white hair, and wearing well-worn work clothes greets you in his Croatian accent. It's just Milan Matulich, the winemaker and co-owner.

There's something very special about Dobra Zemlja wines—perhaps it's the fact that the vineyards

Dobra's inviting wine cave and tasting room

surrounding the tasting room and winery are in line with "green" thinking. Matulich shies away from using chemical pesticides and fertilizers, and his vines are thriving—all 17 acres of them. He prefers to, as he says, "Leave my grapes unmolested."

Matulich, his wife Victoria, and Mike Daugherty opened the winery in 1995. Located on 50 acres of land that in the mid-19th century was home to a hydraulic gold mining operation, and later an Angora goat farm, Matulich named his new home and winery Dobra Zemlja, Croatian for "good earth." His wines tell the tale of Matulich's love for winemaking and his eastern European upbringing. He grew up drinking wine; in his native land, even the kids drank Zinfandel, usually diluted with water. His wines are amazingly robust, tasty, and have a high alcohol content. To learn more about Matulich, read his winemaker interview at **www.WineOhGuide.com**.

The winery is inside a restored 19th-century building. Below the building, but accessible from the front, is the tasting room and wine cave, which offers the perfect climate for storing oak wine barrels. Outside, there are numerous picnic tables scattered beneath trees in a parklike setting, with views of a pond. To the right of the tasting room, behind some work sheds, is a 120-year-old California black walnut, thought to be the state's biggest and tallest.

While all of their wines are amazing—especially the Barbera and Zinfandel—one of the more popular and whimsical favorites is Milan Ruz, a blend of Syrah and Zin grapes. The wine comes in a glass jug with a screw cap (with a cork underneath). It's an absolutely wonderful wine, and if you bring your old jugs back, they will refill them at a discounted price. Keep in mind that they can't be recorked, thus the wine will have to be consumed within a few days—a real bummer, huh? For you more conservative wine drinkers, you can purchase the same wine in a standard wine bottle. It tastes just as good, but is not as much fun.

FEATURED WINES: Sangiovese, Barbera, Syrah, and Zinfandel
TASTING COST: Complimentary
HOURS: Daily, 10 AM–5 PM
LOCATION: 12505 Steiner Road, Plymouth
PHONE: 209-245-3183
WEBSITE: www.dobraz.com

11 *Jeff Runquist Wines*

It can be said that Jeff Runquist, winemaker and co-owner of Jeff Runquist Wines, is a modest man. While some may feel this is a bold statement, if you learn about Runquist and his winemaking practices, it is a fitting conclusion; Runquist publicly gives credit to the grape growers he uses (he buys all of his grapes). His homage to those growers can be found on his wine labels. In a profile from a 2005 interview for *Vineyard & Winery Management*, Runquist states, "I'm willing to give growers the kudos they deserve, so the grower's name appears on the label, and it appears before mine. It all goes back to playing the game the way I want to play it."

In pursuit of the right grapes, Runquist, a University of California at Davis graduate in fermentation science (now referred to as "enology"), travels throughout the Golden State. Making no more than 4,500 cases a year, Runquist noted, "We work very hard to produce balanced wines—wines that will age and become more complex with time, but wines that can also be enjoyed in their youth . . . Once I release a new vintage I rarely return to the previous year's wine. My father [Jim] likes that; it means more of the older wines for him."

The winery opened in 1995, and all the offerings are red. There are no sweet or white wines here. The tasting room is sophisticated and polished, just like Runquist's

Tasting room at Jeff Runquist Wines

wine and his staff. At the helm of the tasting room is the other half of the successful Runquist team—Jeff's wife Margie, who "keeps it all running" according to her husband. The knowledgeable tasting room team includes Runquist's aforementioned father Jim, who, according to his son, "loves to tell embarrassing stories about the winemaker!" And not to be left out of the fun is Jeff's mom Kay, who jumps behind the tasting counter when things get busy. You trivia nuts should check out Runquist's online wine quiz. It's great fun!

FEATURED WINES: Petite Sirah and Barbera
TASTING COST: Complimentary
HOURS: Friday, 12 PM–5 PM; Saturday and Sunday, 11 AM–5 PM
LOCATION: 10776 Shenandoah Road, Plymouth
PHONE: 209-245-6282
WEBSITE: www.jeffrunquistwines.com

12 *Karly Wines*

Karly Wines has been an institution in the Amador County winemaking industry since 1980. Located on Bell Road, the winery is a short drive off the main road. When you pull into the winery, you'll probably do a double-take as the tasting room building blends in with the landscaping and can be hard to see at first. It's so nondescript that a sign hangs over the front announcing the entrance, and another sign near the door greets you: No, REALLY—THIS IS THE TASTING ROOM.

While the outside may be unremarkable, stepping into the tasting room is like walking into your best friend's country kitchen. There's a refrigerator, dishwasher, microwave, and other kitchen necessities and appliances, including a wonderful six-burner, cast-iron gas stove. Perched on top of this ageless appliance is a fun collection of old-fashioned enamel coffee and tea pots. In the middle of the "kitchen" is a long island, which serves as the tasting bar. Here, friendly staff tend to their customers, keeping the wine flowing and the conversation upbeat and fun—we all know that whenever anyone hosts a party in their home, everyone usually ends up in the kitchen!

Founders, owners, and veteran vintners Buck and Karly Cobb are well regarded in the wine business. Prior to opening a winery, Buck was a fighter pilot in the Korean War, a nuclear engineer at Lawrence Livermore

Sign at Karly

Laboratory, and a state bureaucrat. And the winery's name is, of course, attributable to Mrs. Cobb: When asked about it, Buck explained that he chose Karly to "secure [my] wife's enthusiastic participation."

Karly Wines is legendary for their Zinfandels, and with one sip, you'll know why. What started out as one of the first boutique wineries in Amador County now produces upward of 10,000 cases annually. The Cobb's son Garth and his wife Jonna are part of the business and opened Bantam Cellars (see page 180), on Shenandoah Road, in 2007. And according to the family, the

WINE MYTH } More money gets you more enjoyable wine.
    —Buck Cobb

third generation of Cobb winemakers will be starting college soon. Commenting about his winery and any additional services it provides, such as a picnic area or wedding space, Buck Cobb was short in his response: "None, just damn good wine." He couldn't be more right.

FEATURED WINE: Zinfandel
TASTING COST: Complimentary
HOURS: Daily, 12 PM–4 PM
LOCATION: 11076 Bell Road, Plymouth
PHONE: 800-654-0880 or 209-245-3922
WEBSITE: www.karlywines.com

---

13 *Nine Gables Vineyard and Winery*

Perched atop a hill just off of Shenandoah Road is Nine Gables Vineyard and Winery. It is also the site of the Old Peroni Ranch; the family, who settled in the valley more than a century ago, planted Zinfandel and Mission grapes, as well as walnut trees. Many of the original walnut trees and a few of the Mission grapevines still grow near the current tasting room and picnic area.

According to the winery's website, records indicate the old farmhouse, which is still standing west of Nine Gables, was built in 1857 (built either by the Peronis or by earlier settlers). The Peronis also had a winery

A few of Nine Gables's award-winning wines

on-site, which no longer exists. The winery closed its doors before World War II, and the 120-acre ranch was parceled out.

Winery owners Jerry and Pamela Notestine purchased the property in the 1980s. They built their nine-gabled home, which sits directly behind the winery and is its namesake, in 1992. Just six years later, they released their first wine. A self-taught winemaker, Jerry has taken 30 classes over the years at the University of California at Davis and is now teaching the couple's son Ryan. Their wines are produced by hand and typically stay in oak barrels for 18 months before bottling.

Nine Gables is one of the smaller wineries on Shenandoah Road, and the Notestines plan to keep it that way. When asked what makes their wine special,

Jerry answered that they make "small batch natural fermentations with mostly estate-grown grapes." Considering their small operation, what's pleasantly surprising is the breadth of their wine list, from Chardonnay and champagne to myriad huge red wines and even a Mission sherry, which is said to be scrumptious.

WINE MYTH } Wine gets better with age; actually it's that wine changes with age. **—Jerry Notestine**

When visiting, don't be surprised if you're approached by one of the winery dogs, Lucky or Blue. Also don't miss the very interesting fountain in the picnic area; it's a magnum-sized wine bottle! And if you don't want to head home right away, you can stay at the Notestines' new bed-and-breakfast, found above the tasting room. As the Notestines describe it, "Although we do not intend on serving breakfast, we are trying to get people to think of 'B&B' as 'Bed and Bottle.'"

FEATURED WINE: Mission
TASTING COST: Complimentary
HOURS: Monday–Wednesday, 11 AM–4 PM; Thursday–Sunday, 11 AM–5 PM
LOCATION: 10778 Shenandoah Road, Plymouth
PHONE: 209-245-3949
WEBSITE: www.9gables.com

14 *Renwood Winery*

If you're a fan of Amador County wines, then you already know that "All roads lead to Renwood." While many may think the winery's slogan is pretentious, Renwood Winery is known the world over and has created many of California's most unique wines. And even though Renwood hails from what is considered by many in the business to be a small wine region, the winery definitely runs with the big dogs of the Golden State's multibillion dollar wine industry. It even leads the pack with its exquisite flagship wine, Grandpère Zinfandel, taken from the oldest clone of Zinfandel vine in the U.S.

Renwood is the heart, soul, and joy of founder Robert Smerling. A Boston native, Smerling, a man with a diverse background and many talents, wanted to add "winery owner" to his list of accomplishments. He chose Amador County as his base and opened Renwood in 1993, making 2,500 cases that year. Renwood now produces more than 100,000 cases annually, with distribution all over the world. Even more amazing is that all of Renwood's grapes are handpicked and sorted; the logistics of such an endeavor would boggle the mind of even the most dedicated winemaker. Smerling thrives on challenges and demands only the best of the best for his customers; to learn more about Smerling, read his interview at **www.WineOhGuide.com.**

Renwood's showcase tasting room

According to Smerling, he named the winery in honor of his wife Rene (pronounced REE-nee), with the wren becoming part of the company's successful brand. Since the winery's name begins with an "r" instead of a "w," as in the spelling of the bird, Smerling said he receives corrections from people all the time. "My favorite story is about my daughter. She was in the second or third grade and we got called to the principal's office. We were shocked because Sarah had thrown a temper tantrum in class. When I saw Sarah, I asked her what happened. She said, 'Oh, the teacher's stupid. She spelled wren with a 'w' and I tried to correct her.'"

As Amador County's largest producer of wine, Renwood bottles nearly two dozen selections, including two proprietary wines and some decadent dessert wines, such as their Colheita Port, a rare tawny port aged for 10 years. Another dessert wine that is a hit is Renwood's Amador Ice. Served chilled, it is instantly refreshing—the aroma alone will intrigue your senses.

But the granddaddy of them all, without comparison, is Renwood's Grandpère Zinfandel. A proprietary brand, the grapes are from the oldest clone of Zinfandel in the U.S. Dating back to the 1860s, the vineyard is located behind the winery. This unique clone, which produces a big, spicy Zin grape, is planted on its own rootstock and is classically head pruned. For those not up on their French, *grandpère* means "grandfather," an apropos title regarding the wine's stature in the industry.

While Renwood's tasting room may look small from the outside, you'll be pleasantly surprised upon entering. The tasting area is spacious and elegant, and their enthusiastic staff is helpful and eager to please. With wine in hand, you're invited to roam; be sure to visit the gift area, where their selection of imported items is amazing. The winery has a small "grab-and-go" selection of gourmet cheese and meat items, and you can enjoy a quiet picnic just outside in their lush courtyard setting. Cigar lovers should check out Renwood's signature collection; these elegant cigars are handcrafted with a special blend of Dominican binders and fillers, wrapped in high-grade Connecticut Shade paper.

Near the gift area is Renwood's Heritage Room, where special events and pourings take place. If the doors are open, check out the historic photos that line the walls; you'll see winemaking the old-fashioned way! And here's a bit of trivia: If you look up at the Heritage Room's doorway before entering, you'll see a gorgeous and ornate wooden doorframe. That's the fireplace mantle from Nevada's infamous Mustang Ranch. Smerling just grinned when asked how he got his hands on it!

FEATURED WINES: Zinfandel and Italian and Rhone varietals
TASTING COST: Complimentary
HOURS: Daily, 10:30 AM–5:30 PM
LOCATION: 12225 Steiner Road, Plymouth
PHONE: 800-348-VINO (8466) or 209-245-6979
WEBSITE: www.renwood.com

15 *Shenandoah Vineyards*

When Shirley and Leon Sobon purchased the old Steiner Ranch in 1977, the Silicon Valley couple was following their dream, with their six children in tow. A senior scientist with Lockheed Research Lab, Leon wanted to "find a new expression for my chemical and engineering background, and to take my love for growing things and making wine—as a hobby—to a new level," he shared. The Sobons converted the old ranch into their winery and named it after the valley they overlook. Upon opening, Shenandoah Vineyards became the third winery in the Shenandoah Valley appellation; more than 30 years later, they now produce upward of 30,000 cases a year, using only their own organically grown grapes.

Shenandoah Vineyards has brought in award after award for their wines, and Leon Sobon is recognized as a leader in the winemaking industry (he also owns the historic Sobon Estate—see page 212). His son Paul, who grew up at the winery, is now an accomplished winemaker just like his dad. Educated at the University of California at Davis, Paul traveled extensively through the wine regions of Europe and Australia learning the business and even studied with Vincent Fabre of Chateau Lamothe Cissac in Bordeaux, France, and Stuart Anderson of Balgownie Winery in southeastern Australia. "Paul was my assistant for 30 years," said Leon, explaining that his son took over the winemaking role three years ago. "The wines are better and sales have never been so good. I guess I'll have to admit [this] to him soon!"

Being respectful of the environment is a high priority for the Sobon family. At Shenandoah Vineyards, the roof of both the winery production facility and part of the tasting room support a 50-kilowatt photovoltaic solar system that provides electricity for the entire operation. They also recycle all of their cardboard, glass, and metal waste, and shred about 10 cubic feet of white paper waste from their office every week, adding it to their grape compost. According to Leon, their carbon footprint has diminished to the point that they are carbon neutral.

Located on a knoll, Shenandoah Vineyards's tasting room was once an old stone garage. The building looks small from the outside, but when you enter, you will be astounded by its expansive interior. Besides the winery's outstanding wines, the tasting room hosts a large professional art gallery, with some pieces for sale, and a new show rotates through every few months. If you like to cook, be sure to check out the recipe book in the tasting area; a three-inch-thick binder, the book features recipes that pair well with Shenandoah's wines. Behind each recipe are extra copies for visitors to take. Outside, you'll find a well-shaded picnic area with views of the winery's namesake valley, perfect for a lazy afternoon lunch and glass of wine.

Shenandoah's expansive tasting room and gallery

The fact that the Sobon family has two wineries in Plymouth is a plus for their customers. Even though tasting is complimentary at both places, for a $5 fee, you can buy a wine glass at either winery and then taste reserve wines at both places. Considering that both offer superb wines, this may be one of the best deals in the region!

FEATURED WINE: Zinfandel
TASTING COST: Complimentary
HOURS: Daily, 10 AM–5 PM
LOCATION: 12300 Steiner Road, Plymouth
PHONE: 209-245-4455
WEBSITE: www.sobonwine.com

16 *Sobon Estate*

Leon and Shirley Sobon, owners of Shenandoah Vineyards (see page 209), purchased the D'Agostini Winery from that family in 1989 to celebrate their 30th wedding anniversary. They reopened as Sobon Estate winery a year later.

The winery was originally founded in 1856 by Swiss immigrant Adam Uhlinger, who named it after himself. The Uhlinger Winery was one of the first commercial wineries in the state, making Uhlinger the pioneer of winemaking in the region; he planted some of the first Zinfandel vines in Shenandoah Valley. The Uhlinger ranch house is next to the Sobon Estate tasting room. The downstairs section, made up of stone from the vineyard, was the winery, and the family lived upstairs.

Uhlinger continued his strong tradition of winemaking until Enrico D'Agostini purchased the winery and its 125 acres in 1911. D'Agostini worked the land and built a name for himself and his wines. When Prohibition was enacted in 1920, the D'Agostini family was able to keep the winery open by selling fresh grapes and wine for religious services, returning to full-fledged winemaking when the ban was lifted in 1933. As such, the Uhlinger/D'Agostini/Sobon winery is the oldest continuously operated winery in the Golden State.

Fully aware of the vast history of their winery, and the fact that their winery is a California Registered

Tasting room (left) and original winery and home (right)

Historical Landmark, the Sobons have done an excellent job honoring both the Uhlinger and D'Agostini families. A memorable museum can be found in the original winery building, where local wine history is shared, along with artifacts from the early days of winemaking and agriculture in the state (1860–1920). There is no charge to visit the museum.

The Sobon Estate has more than 85 acres of vineyards, including their famed Cougar Hill and Rocky Top vineyards. Even though Uhlinger's original Zinfandel vines are no longer in existence, portions of the vineyard are 70 to 80 years old, according to son Robert Sobon, the company's business systems manager. As with their sister winery Shenandoah Vineyards, Sobon Estate is organically farmed. To learn more about their winemaker Paul Sobon, please see the Shenandoah Vineyards listing.

WINE MYTH } Screw caps are for cheap wine. **—Leon Sobon**

The tasting room at Sobon is warm and inviting, and they have historical books and cookbooks galore! A recipe book in the tasting area features recipes that pair well with Sobon's wines, and behind each recipe are extra copies for visitors to take. The picnic grounds at Sobon are always busy, so get there early to find a shady spot under their 100-year-old fig tree.

The fact that the Sobon family owns this winery and Shenandoah is a plus for their customers. Even though complimentary tasting is offered at both places, for a $5 fee you can buy a wine glass and taste, at no charge, from each of the winery's reserve lists.

FEATURED WINE: Zinfandel
TASTING COST: Complimentary
HOURS: Daily, 10 AM–5 PM
LOCATION: 14430 Shenandoah Road, Plymouth
PHONE: 209-245-6554
WEBSITE: www.sobonwine.com

17 *Stonehouse Vineyards and Winery*

Wine and art are a fine mix, especially at Stonehouse Vineyards and Winery. First, the wine: According to owner and winemaker Mitchell B. Shultz, his wines are true varietals. "We do not blend our wines, we tend to use tried-and-true methods and all of our varietals are 100 percent what is on the label." Shultz noted that only once have they blended a wine, Mikayla's Cuvee, named for his daughter Mikayla.

Second, the art, thanks to painter Thomas Kinkade. Entering the winery's large, modern tasting room, you'll find Kinkade's work throughout, which is a wonderful complement to Stonehouse's great estate wines. "Kinkade is a personal friend and we are, and will be, the only winery with a Thomas Kinkade gallery," explained Shultz. He noted that a major winery expansion to include a Thomas Kinkade–style wedding chapel is in the works.

Shultz became interested in wine as a young man. He grew up in Sonoma County and worked at many wineries owned by family friends. When asked how he ended up in Amador County, Shultz responded: "I saw great potential to be part of the ground floor in an up-and-coming wine region." Shultz's three young children, Matthew, Morgan and Mikayla, help out at the winery, from day-to-day operations to special events. When asked about his family, Shultz said, "The word

Stonehouse's tasting room and Thomas Kinkade gallery

legacy appears on our flagship wines; Cabernet Sauvignon Legacy was created to honor my late father . . . I want to continue that legacy and pass this winery onto all three of my children."

While wine tasting is complimentary, there is a $5 charge to taste two of Stonehouse's reserve wines, served in a fine etched-crystal glass which is yours to keep.

FEATURED WINES: Cabernet Sauvignon and Viognier
TASTING COST: Complimentary
HOURS: Friday–Sunday, 11 AM–5 PM
LOCATION: 10861 Shenandoah Road, Plymouth
PHONE: 209-245-6888
WEBSITE: www.stonehousewines.com

18 *Story Winery*

While much at Story Winery is very old, the same cannot be said about the youthfulness and vibrancy of co-owners Bruce and Jan Tichenor's wines. Here are those "old" numbers; the winery was established by Ann and Gene Story in 1973; the vines by the creek were planted in 1936 and the Mission grapes on the hill were planted about a century ago; the tasting room is a refurbished 120-year-old bunkhouse; and the oak trees that canopy this mountaintop winery are said to be more than 200 years old.

But when you look around, age isn't why Story Winery is worth the drive up Bell Road. Here you'll find a vibrant staff eager to pour you several tastes in their small tasting room, and outside, whimsical metal sculptures, including giant insects and even a full-sized giraffe, will bring a smile to your face. While enjoying your wine, you can take in views of the Cosumnes River Canyon and Story's 40-plus acres of grapes. If nature calls, you'll be treated to a very artistic Porta-Potty (you're on your own for that one). But, most important, you'll see the twinkle in the eyes of both Bruce and Jan as a result of fulfilling their lifelong dreams of owning a winery.

WINE MYTH } To enjoy fine wine you have to be a wine connoisseur. Not true—you just have to know what you like! —Jan Tichenor

TASTING ROOM
BARREL ROOM
PICNIC GROUNDS
BEWARE OF RATTLESNAKES
STORY WINES ONLY please

Retired pharmacists from the Bay Area, the couple purchased the winery from Ann Story Ousley in 1992. "We're living our passion, making luscious Zinfandels," said Jan, and do they make some Zins! Just take one look at their wine list—which is extensive for such a small winery—and you'll see quite an assortment of Zinfandel offerings. And even their website is Zin-based: www.zin.com.

Off the beaten path of Shenandoah Valley proper, the winery is a refreshing respite and a relaxing spot to enjoy a picnic and great wine. For music lovers, Story hosts a summer music series Memorial Day through Labor Day. They also have a fun movie on their website, which is both endearing and informative.

FEATURED WINE: Zinfandel
TASTING COST: Complimentary
HOURS: Daily, 11 AM–5 PM
LOCATION: 10525 Bell Road, Plymouth
PHONE: 800-713-6390 or 209-245-6208
WEBSITE: www.zin.com

Whimsical Story Winery signpost

19 *Terra d'Oro Winery*

Terra d'Oro Winery, formerly Montevina, has been in the Shenandoah Valley for more than three decades. The winery was the first new wine producer in Amador County to open after Prohibition was repealed in 1933. It's hard to believe that nearly 40 years went by before this exemplary wine region returned to its winemaking roots; imagine what the region would be like today if Prohibition never occurred.

Montevina was founded by Cary Gott, Vicki Gott, and W. H. Fields in 1973. About 10 years later, the Gotts left and Fields took over, hiring Jeff Myers as winemaker. In 1987 the winery was sold to the Trinchero family and Myers stayed on as winemaker. If the Trinchero name is not familiar to you, Napa Valley's "Sutter Home" label probably rings a bell. Brothers John and Mario Trinchero purchased the Napa winery in 1948 and kept production small for years. Then in 1968, Mario's oldest son Louis "Bob" Trinchero tried some homemade Zinfandel made from Sierra foothill grapes. Impressed with the varietal, Sutter Home started using Amador County Zinfandel grapes.

It wasn't until 1975 when, purely by accident, White Zinfandel was discovered. According to a 2003 article by Linda Murphy in the *San Francisco Chronicle* (July 2003), "as some 1000 gallons of bleed-off juice from

Terra d'Oro Winery

red Zinfandel refused to ferment to dryness, retaining a substantial amount of sugar, [Bob] Trinchero put the wine aside for the time. He said, 'Two weeks later, I tasted that wine and it was sweet, had a pink color, and I thought, 'Darn, that's pretty good. We bottled it, and the rest is history.'" Sutter Home is now one of the largest, independent, family-run wineries in the nation, and the largest producer of White Zinfandel.

In January 2009, the Trincheros changed the winery name to Terra d'Oro, Spanish for "land of gold." Myers, who is now vice president and general manager, explained that this was done because the Montevina portfolio had branched out to different varietals, none of which were from the county. "On the other hand," he explained, "Terra d'Oro remains steadfastly an Amador County brand. The feeling was that the name of the facility should be reflective of the brand that represents the area."

WINE MYTH } Red wine gives you a hangover. Ah, no . . . alcohol gives you a hangover! **—Jeff Meyers**

With Myers in upper management, winemaker Chris Leamy now oversees the wine production. The affable Leamy, who was schooled at the University of California at Davis and has been at the winery since 2000, is like a kid in a candy store when it comes to the winery's 64,000-square-foot production facility (to learn more about Leamy, read his winemaker interview at **www.WineOhGuide.com**). And the rumor is that Leamy dyes his hair purple every year for harvest. "He's tall and very funny," noted Myers about his replacement. "Oh, he also makes great wine!"

You can see Leamy's "playground" for yourself during one of two tours offered through Terra d'Oro's state-of-the-art, drop-dead-immaculate production facility. Complimentary tours are offered Friday through Sundays at both noon and 2 PM. The winery's tasting room is open daily, and besides featuring their outstanding wines, including their single vineyard Zinfandels, you'll also find an extensive selection of gifts and Terra d'Oro logo items.

FEATURED WINE: Zinfandel
TASTING COST: Complimentary
HOURS: Daily, 10 AM–4:30 PM
LOCATION: 20680 Shenandoah School Road, Plymouth
PHONE: 209-245-6942
WEBSITE: www.terradorowinery.com

---

20 *Terre Rouge and Easton Wines*

Bill Easton, owner and winemaker of Terre Rouge and Easton Wines, is a man of the earth. "I had a passion for wine—the varying terroirs of the Sierra foothills reminded me of many of my favorite European vineyard areas," Easton confided when asked why he started his winery in 1985. An established figure and expert since the mid-1970s in everything having to do with the wine business, Easton has been a wine retailer, wine importer, and vineyard and winemaking consultant.

Easton's sage sense of the art form has served him well, as his winery is endlessly busy. When asked what makes his wine special, he says that no expense is spared and quality comes first, evident when tasting his superb wines, which number nearly two dozen strong. His estate includes a portion of the old Dickson Vineyards, with Zinfandel vines that date back to the 1920s.

As noted, Easton offers two labels, the self-named Easton label and Terre Rouge. The latter focuses on

Tasting room for Terre Rouge and Easton Wines

Rhone varietals that grow in the rugged terroirs of the area (largely granite and volcanic based), while the Easton label is based on non-Rhone varietals, showcasing grapes that work best in Amador County. Per Easton, his winery is the first in the Sierra foothills to make a limited production wine (Syrah) that receives international press every year.

Easton's wife and business partner is Jane O'Riordan, a teacher, cookbook author, and frequent television guest chef. O'Riordan's passion is how wine and food connects people in social settings. "For me, wine is an integral part of daily meals. Our wines are made to complement food, which sounds so obvious, but in California [this is] something often overlooked," explained O'Riordan.

"We have a more European palate when it comes to wine style, coming from many years of traveling there." She is currently working on her second cookbook; you can check out O'Riordan's recipes on the winery's website, under the heading "Jane's Kitchen."

The property at Terre Rouge and Easton is absolutely gorgeous. Inside the Mediterranean-style tasting room you'll find lots of attractive wood, lovely tiled floors, gourmet kitchenware and gifts, myriad cookbooks, and an expansive and inviting tasting bar (remember, this winery is very popular!). Easton suggests sipping some wine with tasting room manager Doug Bellamy, who has been in the business for more than 30 years. Easton said he's "a knowledgeable guy" and that the tasting is "educational, in a fun way." Outside is a patio shaded by a grape arbor perfect for picnicking, and be sure not to miss the petanque court where you can play boules, the French version of Italy's bocce ball.

FEATURED WINES: Zinfandel and Syrah
TASTING COST: Complimentary
HOURS: Friday–Monday, 11 AM–4 PM
LOCATION: 10801 Dickson Road, Plymouth
PHONE: 888 419-1916 or 209-245-4277
WEBSITE: www.terrerougewines.com

21 *TKC Vineyards*

To be the "employee of the month" at TKC Vineyards, you have to have four legs to be considered. But we'll save that story for later. Harold and Monica Nuffer opened TKC Vineyards because, according to Monica, her husband's hobby "got out of control."

In the 1970s, Harold was a home winemaker and also a rocket scientist, and the family lived in California's eastern Sierra Nevada near China Lake's Naval Air Weapons Station where both Harold and Monica worked. The couple purchased property in Amador County as a retirement investment with the thought of opening a winery, and in 1981, they made their dream come true. For several years, Harold completed the long commute from China Lake to the winery—460 miles one way—once a month; the family called the trek his "vacation." Harold finally retired in 1986 and hung up his commuting hat for good.

When it came to selecting the winery's name, the Nuffers had difficulty. With nearly 60 names picked out, they were still stuck. That's when Monica suggested that they name the winery "TKC" after their three daughters, Tierre, Karina, and Courtnay, and Harold agreed. Middle daughter Karina is following in her parent's footsteps, working at the winery full-time. "It is great to have Karina so totally involved in the every day operations," shared her proud mom. "She got her degree in enology at California State University at Fresno, and she brings a lot of great information to our operation."

TKC is small in comparison to others in the valley, but that hasn't stopped the Nuffers from putting out a quality product year after year. They make only red wines in their combination winery, barrel, and tasting room. Since it's a working winery, their visitors can view the operation and taste at the same time. Monica is more honest when it comes to the size of their winery: "We are very small, making approximately 600–1,000 cases a year. Most wineries spill more than we make."

WINE MYTH } **I don't believe in pairing wine with food. If you like the wine and you like the food, you will have a great meal or snack. —Monica Nuffer**

Now about that employee-of-the-month story; this award, granted in perpetuity, has been bestowed upon the Nuffers' winery dog, "D-O-G." That's right, D-O-G's name is pronounced by spelling it. A Norwegian elkhound-shepherd mix, D-O-G is 15 years young. Prior to her arrival, their cockapoo, Boomer, was the official and perpetual "employee of the month" (a cockapoo is a cross between a cocker spaniel and poodle, usually a miniature or toy poodle). But being the gracious big brother, and getting on in years, Boomer turned the title over to D-O-G. "He taught her everything she needed to know about the job," said Monica. "D-O-G took over the heavy responsibility of the job and has excelled!" D-O-G has done so well that

Courtesy of TKC Vineyards

D-O-G hard at work!

she has a wine in her name; D-O-G Private Reserve sports a label featuring its namesake driving the winery's tractor. No, really, she's got her paws on the steering wheel and a grin on her face. And D-O-G's wine is one of TKC's most popular offerings. If you're lucky, maybe D-O-G will pose for a photo with you when you visit—Monica said that their celebrity canine loves the paparazzi!

FEATURED WINES: Zinfandel and Cabernet Sauvignon
TASTING COST: Complimentary
HOURS: Saturday, 11 AM–5 PM; Sunday, 1 PM–5 PM
LOCATION: 11001 Valley Drive, Plymouth
PHONE: 888-627-2356 or 209-245-6428
WEBSITE: www.tkcvineyards.com

22 *Wilderotter Vineyard and Winery*

Wilderotter Vineyard began in the 1990s, with their first harvest in 2001 and subsequent release of that vintage in 2003. Shortly thereafter, they became Wilderotter Vineyard and Winery. "Opening a winery was a natural progression from growing grapes," explained co-owner Jay Wilderotter when asked why he started his business, noting that with the increase of wine production and customer traffic, it made sense to do so. Located on Shenandoah School Road, Wilderotter produces 3,000 cases a year.

Jay and his wife Maggie fell in love with Amador County when they began their "search for 'Grape land'" many years ago. They purchased 40 acres and with the help of courses at the University of California at Davis in viticulture and enology, Jay planted and nurtured his vineyard, becoming a premier grape grower in the region. After six years of selling their fruit to other wineries, the couple opened their own tasting room with great success.

WINE MYTH } Wine is 80 percent water. —**Jay Wilderotter**

The tasting room itself is reminiscent of Italian-style architecture. Jay explained, "We have a well-built Tuscan-style tasting room with a lot of character, and a fantastic staff that enjoy what they do." There are two

Wilderotter's tasting room

tasting areas inside, and inviting outdoor seating areas, some with umbrellas, in both the front and back.

FEATURED WINES: Sauvignon Blanc, Zinfandel, Barbera, and Syrah
TASTING COST: Complimentary
HOURS: Friday–Sunday, 10:30 AM–5 PM; Monday and Thursday, 11 AM–4 PM
LOCATION: 19890 Shenandoah School Road, Plymouth
PHONE: 209-245-6016
WEBSITE: www.wilderottervineyard.com

SUTTER CREEK

23 *Avio Vineyards*

At Avio Vineyards, owners Lisa and Stefano Watson transformed their way of life and opened their business *per l'amore di famiglia,* Italian for "for the love of family." The Watsons' story of how they ended up in Sutter Creek is compelling. Here's an abbreviated version (the full story is on their website): Prior to opening Avio in 2003, the couple was working in Atlanta, Georgia, in marketing and sales positions. They traveled extensively, spending the majority of their time on airplanes. While they knew they wanted to do something else with their lives one day, they never settled on any one thing. Then the terrorist attacks happened on September 11, 2001. "As with many people, this horrific event caused self-reflection and intense introspection with regard to the way we were spending our precious gift of life," Lisa writes. Born and raised in the small town of Avio, Italy, Lisa hailed from generations of winemakers. Whenever they visited Avio, the couple noticed how happy everyone was and how the art of winemaking was a family affair. They decided that they wanted to go into the family business. After learning everything they could, they purchased the nearly 80 acres where their winery and home now stand.

A few of Avio Vineyards's award-winning wines

Making such a drastic lifestyle change can be both scary and trying, but the Watsons enjoy and savor each and every day. When asked about their favorite aspect of owning and running a winery, Lisa answered, "The nightly 'quality control' check of all our wines!" It's obvious that this highly successful husband and wife team revel in their new life; when asked about working with family, a very witty Lisa responded, "We are a husband-and-wife team. The thing I look forward to the most is sleeping with the boss!"

To honor their Italian roots, the Watsons have broken down their 30 acres of vineyards into five blocks, naming four after Italian uncles (Nino, Giorgio, Giancarlo, and Paulino), and one after Lisa's mother Milena.

They also have the only estate-grown Pinot Grigio in the county. And to come full circle with their love of family, the couple, who have no children, created "Avio's Ark," taking in unwanted and rescued animals. Here's a quick list: winery and barn cats, goats, llamas, a horse, mallard and Indian runner ducks, guinea hens, domestic hens, roosters, peacocks, sheep, a Dutch bunny, and Avio Vineyards's official greeter—Tux the dog.

WINE MYTH } **It isn't evaporation that causes the wine to slowly disappear in the barrels; it's the angels drinking their share! —Stefano Watson**

Their tasting room is Tuscan-style (of course!) and a large L-shaped tasting bar means there's plenty of room for everyone. If the tasting room isn't too busy, ask for a tour of the grounds; you'll see the botanical gardens, vineyards, and the amazing view from the back of the property. And if you're really lucky, they may give you a tour of the Carriage House. A one room guest lodge, this upscale authentic Western-themed room is luxury and privacy at its finest; you can relax and enjoy wine or champagne by the pool or even be winemaker for a day.

FEATURED WINES: Sangiovese, Pinot Grigio, and Zinfandel
TASTING COST: Complimentary
HOURS: Friday–Sunday, 11 AM–5 PM
LOCATION: 14520 Ridge Road, Sutter Creek
PHONE: 209-267-1515
WEBSITE: www.aviowine.com

24 *Sierra Ridge Vineyards and Winery*

Sierra Ridge Vineyards and Winery, on historic Ridge Road south of Sutter Creek, welcomes you to the Mother Lode, "where gold is not the only treasure." The John Bree family purchased 357 acres of pristine land in 1988 and established a vineyard and winery. At an elevation of 2000 feet, their vineyard—now 170 acres strong—hosts more than two dozen varietals, including Pinotage, their flagship grape and wine. A hybrid grape from South Africa, Pinotage is gaining favor with wine lovers. Besides being the first in the nation to grow the grape, Sierra Ridge Vineyard is also one of the largest producers of the fruit in the U.S.

John Bree is a third-generation winemaker, and his adult children—son John L. Bree and daughter Gretchen Brown—carry on the family legacy. The senior Bree is a University of California at Davis graduate and has been in the wine business for 50-plus years. The family's wines are mostly estate-produced, with the exception of their Zinfandel, which comes from another vineyard the family developed and now manages.

The winery's tasting room is small and quaint, but their dazzling wines make up for this! Outside you'll find a covered picnic area and two bocce ball courts for those who would like to mix tasting with some exercise. For those who want even more exercise, arrangements can be made with the winery for access to

Sierra Ridge's tasting room and winery

the 1860s homestead on the property, a 1.5-mile hike down a dirt road.

According to Eric Costa, Sierra Ridge's winemaker and also an author and historian, the property, which was registered in a claim dated 1857, was a large agricultural partnership that included Paul Devoto. The property was referred to as Italian's Ranch and was used for fruit growing and winemaking. Along with other buildings, a stone house (the one that stands in ruins today) was constructed. Portions of the property went through different legal agreements, and it wasn't until 1902 that ownership was transferred to another Devoto family member. Eventually Earnest Digitale, who came to Amador County in 1899, purchased the property in the 1930s and operated a cattle ranch until his death in 1953. Besides the ruins of the stone house and winery, other surviving remnants of the pioneer occupation at Sierra Ridge include rock terracing, a large century-old fig tree, heirloom roses, and an ancient pear tree.

If you're not quite up to the hike to the original homestead, the winery offers a hayride to the site during spring and summer. The tour, which includes a historical presentation, passes through Sierra Ridge's expansive vineyard. All tours require advance reservations, and the winery can accommodate larger groups; call for costs and details. The winery allows equestrians and mountain bikers on its more than 5 miles of trails—appointments are required to gain access.

FEATURED WINE: Pinotage (a hybrid grape from South Africa)
TASTING COST: Complimentary
HOURS: Summer, Friday–Sunday, 11 AM–5 PM; Winter, Friday–Sunday, 11 AM–4 PM
LOCATION: 14110 Ridge Road, Sutter Creek
PHONE: 209-267-1316
WEBSITE: www.sierraridgewine.com

+ More Area Wineries

DRYTOWN

Drytown Cellars
HOURS: Friday–Sunday, 11 AM–5 PM
LOCATION: 16030 Highway 49, Drytown
PHONE: 866-DRYTOWN (379-8696) or 209-245-3500
WEBSITE: www.drytowncellars.com

IONE

Clos du Lac Cellars
HOURS: Wednesday–Sunday, 10 AM–4 PM
LOCATION: 3151 Highway 88, Ione
PHONE: 209-274-2238
WEBSITE: www.closdulac.com

PLYMOUTH

Karmère Vineyards and Winery
HOURS: Thursday–Monday, 11 AM–5 PM
LOCATION: 11970 Shenandoah Road, Plymouth
PHONE: 209-245-5000
WEBSITE: www.karmere.com

Vino Noceto
HOURS: Weekdays, 11 AM–4 PM; Weekends, 11 AM–5 PM
LOCATION: 11011 Shenandoah Road, Plymouth
PHONE: 877-4NOCETO (466-2386) or 209-245-6556
WEBSITE: www.noceto.com

Young's Vineyards
HOURS: Weekdays, 10 AM–4 PM; Weekends, 10:30 AM–5 PM
LOCATION: 10120 Shenandoah Road, Plymouth
PHONE: 209-245-3005
WEBSITE: www.youngsvineyards.com

SUTTER CREEK

Sutter Creek Wine Tasting
HOURS: Daily, 11 AM–6 PM
LOCATION: 85 Main Street, Sutter Creek
PHONE: 209-267-5838
WEBSITE: www.suttercreekwinetasting.com

SIDE TRIPS

Amador County is a region dotted with small towns and lots of history. For thousands of years before the 49ers arrived on the scene, Native Americans—Miwok, Maidu, and others—lived, traveled, and traded throughout the Sierra Nevada foothills. **Indian Grinding Rock State Historic Park** (www.parks. ca.gov), 8 miles east of Jackson, features more bedrock mortar holes than found anywhere else in the U.S. Among the 1,185 mortar holes is a recreated Miwok village with its ceremonial roundhouse and the **Chaw'se Regional Indian Museum.** There are examples of numerous tribes' basketry, jewelry, feather regalia, and weapons.

Along Highway 49, the few surviving Gold Rush towns offer antique shops, restaurants, and other businesses. **Drytown**—originally called Dry Diggins due to the lack of water, which made placer mining tough, not because liquor was absent—has several 1850s-era buildings to discover. Those that survived the past 150 years or more are usually made of brick; one such structure is thought to have been the mine office of George Hearst, the father of William Randolph Hearst. **Sutter Creek** was named after John Sutter, the founder of Sutter's Fort in Sacramento and owner of the sawmill in Coloma where gold was discovered. Sutter sent a party of men to the area where the town now stands in search of timber for his sawmill. Finding a great stand of sugar pines, the group left Sutter's name attached to a nearby creek. A few years later, Sutter Creek would become a rambunctious Gold Rush town known for revelry and bar fights.

These towns and others, including **Plymouth, Amador City,** and **Volcano** (www.touramador.com/act/), have maintained their ties with historic California. By the way, Volcano got its name from the local miners who thought that because the area was a deep cup-shaped valley, they must be digging for gold inside a volcano. There weren't any volcanoes around, but with the advent of hydraulic mining, thousands of people came to Volcano bringing theaters, bars, brothels, 17 hotels, and more to a short-lived prosperity. You can even see "Old Abe," a small cannon smuggled into town to intimidate local Confederate sympathizers.

If you're not afraid of the dark, a trip into one of the county's three underground adventure areas might be just the ticket. In Volcano you'll find **Black Chasm Cavern** (www.caverntours.com). The cave is known for its vast arrays of rare helictite crystals. Aboveground, visitors can pan for gemstones in flumes just outside the 3,000-square-foot visitor's center. Another venture owned by the same company as Black Chasm is **Sutter Gold Mine** (www.caverntours.com), located outside Sutter Creek. Guided underground tours are given, and everyone participating must wear a hard hat (tours are not recommended for ages 4 and under). The mine offers a look at the gold mining process, from panning to hydraulic mining to hard-rock techniques.

In its rough-and-tumble heyday, **Jackson** was famous for its gold, prostitutes, and gambling. Today the focus is on tourists as the inns, restaurants, and dozens of shops cater to those searching for golden bargains and great times. A little farther south in the town of **Jackson** is the third underground adventure to be found in this region, the famous **Kennedy Mine** (www.kennedygoldmine.com). It was one of California's richest mines, producing more than $28 million in gold (most at $20 per ounce) between 1886 and 1942 when it closed. In 1922, a fire in the adjacent **Argonaut Mine** trapped 42 miners 4650 feet below the surface. Rescue efforts to drill from a nearby Kennedy mine shaft reached the miners, but it was too late to save them.

SIDE TRIPS

For More Information

Amador Vintners' Association
P.O. Box 667
Plymouth, CA 95669
888-655-8614 or 209-245-6992
www.amadorwine.com

Amador Council of Tourism
P.O. Box 40
Sutter Creek, CA 95685
877-868-7262
www.touramador.com

Amador County Chamber of Commerce
P.O. Box 596
571 South Highway 49
Jackson, CA 95642
209-223-0350
www.amadorcountychamber.com

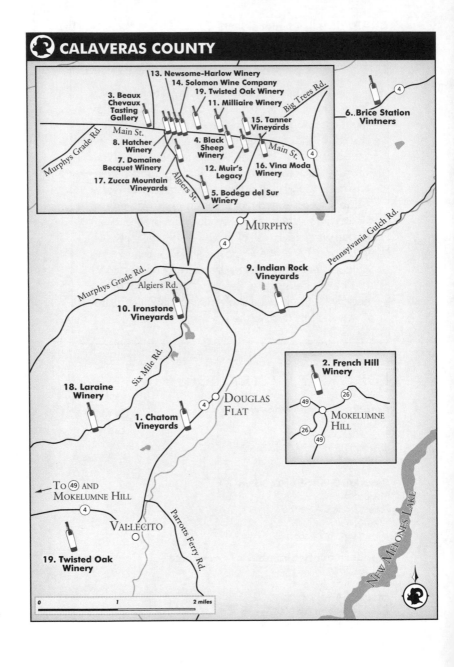

CALAVERAS COUNTY

13. Newsome-Harlow Winery
14. Solomon Wine Company
19. Twisted Oak Winery
11. Milliaire Winery

3. Beaux Chevaux Tasting Gallery

Big Trees Rd.

6. Brice Station Vintners

15. Tanner Vineyards

Main St.

Murphys Grade Rd.

8. Hatcher Winery

4. Black Sheep Winery

Main St.

7. Domaine Becquet Winery

12. Muir's Legacy

16. Vina Moda Winery

17. Zucca Mountain Vineyards

Algiers St.

5. Bodega del Sur Winery

MURPHYS

9. Indian Rock Vineyards

Pennsylvania Gulch Rd.

Murphys Grade Rd.

Algiers Rd.

10. Ironstone Vineyards

Six Mile Rd.

2. French Hill Winery

18. Laraine Winery

1. Chatom Vineyards

DOUGLAS FLAT

49   26

26   49

MOKELUMNE HILL

TO 49 AND MOKELUMNE HILL

VALLECITO

Parrotts Ferry Rd.

NEW MELONES LAKE

19. Twisted Oak Winery

0   1   2 miles

the
Sierra
Foothills

★ Calaveras County

When it comes to history and natural resources, Calaveras County is rich beyond anyone's dreams. Granted, gold was the draw in the 1850s, but those who stayed after the gold ran out just a decade later discovered a plethora of opportunities in this yet untamed land. The Spanish word *calaveras* means "skulls." Spanish army officer Gabriel Moraga, one of the first European explorers in this region during the early 1800s, named the Sierra foothill river he wandered across the Calaveras River because of the many bones he found on its banks. He believed the bones belonged to Indians who had died due to famine or tribal conflicts. The county was officially created during statehood in 1850, even though a few years later parts of it were ceded to Amador and Alpine counties.

Calaveras County is probably best known for a certain story written by a certain author. Mark Twain based his 1865 story "The Celebrated Jumping Frog of Calaveras County" on a yarn he had heard in an Angels

Camp bar. Twain penned the piece in his cabin on Jackass Hill, just north of town (to find out how to visit the cabin, see page 304). The first frog jumping event was held more than 50 years later in 1928 and has become an annual event since.

Natural resources are another big draw in Calaveras County, from Calaveras Big Trees State Park and its giant sequoias to the myriad caverns and gold mines (to learn more, see page 303). But, by far, the agricultural aspect of Calaveras County is the region's biggest draw and is growing every day. There's bound to be several more wineries opening in the county in the near future.

The biggest winery concentration is in the town of Murphys, where more than 15 wineries can be found. The town was named after Irishmen John and Daniel Murphy, brothers who were part of the first group to bring wagons across the rugged Sierra Nevada and into the Sacramento Valley. The year was 1844, and when the Gold Rush hit five years later, they had a jump on all the 49ers because they were already in the state. The brothers first started mining in Vallecito, in an area that became known as Murphys Old Diggings. Then the duo moved closer to what is today historic Murphys; the town was eventually called Murphys. Because they had a head start, the brothers were very successful in their quest: When John left town at the end of 1849—when others were just coming to the area—he had made millions. All in all, about $20 million worth of gold was found in the Murphys area.

DOUGLAS FLAT

1 *Chatom Vineyards*

Located on Highway 4 just 2 miles south of Murphys, Chatom Vineyards is definitely worth the stop. When Gay Chatom, a San Franciscan and fifth-generation Californian, moved by herself to Douglas Flat and the beautiful Esmeralda Valley in the 1980s, many in the area were surprised. Her education and professional career had focused on technology and marketing, and locals questioned her decision to establish a winery in this valley. But determined to start a winery, Chatom was undeterred. Her successful venture now boasts 65 acres of vineyards with 13 major varietals.

There's a fun story behind one of Chatom's popular wine brands: According to their website, since the winery's founder and owner is female and the business is operated mostly by women (even though there has always been a few male employees), Chatom became known as the "female" winery. Staying true to its feminine roots, then winemaker Mari Wells (now with David Girard Vineyards in El Dorado County, see page 124) decided several years ago to make a wine by women, for women, which she called She Wines. The first release was in July 2004. Wells left soon after and

Courtesy of Chatom Vineyards

Chatom's tasting room and winery

current winemaker Mark Kunz (a male—surprise!) came onboard. Embracing the idea of the She Wine brand, he produced the next vintages, which were released in 2005 and 2007. She Red and She White became immediate hits. Today, Chatom donates proceeds from this brand to women's health-related charities — heart disease research for She Red and breast cancer research for She White.

FEATURED WINES: Chardonnay and Syrah
TASTING COST: Complimentary
HOURS: Daily, 11 AM–5 PM
LOCATION: 1969 Highway 4, Douglas Flat
PHONE: 800-435-8852 or 209-736-6500
WEBSITE: www.chatomvineyards.com

MOKELUMNE HILL

2 *French Hill Winery*

Mokelumne Hill (population: almost 800), on Highway 49 near the border of Calaveras and Amador counties, was a booming metropolis during the Gold Rush. It was also one of the richest towns during the 1850s, but with infamous bandit Joaquin Murrieta and other notorious characters in their midst, "Moke Hill" (as the locals called it) soon became known as one of the most violent and bawdy towns in the Mother Lode. While fortune-seekers left in the early 1860s when the gold ran out, many of the town's original buildings are still intact, a testament to visions of prosperity and riches galore.

Four highland areas of Mokelumne Hill were claimed back then—Stockton Hill, Negro Hill, Sport Hill, and French Hill. The latter is home to French Hill Winery, the county's most northern winery. According to their website, French Hill owes its name to the French trappers who roamed the area's red clay and gravelly slopes in the 1840s, but their attention was diverted to gold mining in 1845, three years before the discovery of gold in Coloma. These trappers were ahead of the times.

French Hill's tasting room and winery

Another forward-thinking person is the winery's owner Rod Ruthel. According to Ruthel, his winery was the first in California to be certified by Green-e, the nation's leading independent certification and verification program for renewable energy and greenhouse gas emission reductions in the retail market (www. green-e.org). Keeping the environment in mind, the winery recycles all of their glass and cardboard and relies completely on solar power.

In business since 1999, French Hill offers 20 different varietals for wine lovers. A self-taught winemaker, Ruthel explained why he started his winery: "After 25 years as a wine label designer, I felt there was too much mediocre wine being made. I set out to make ultra-premium wines of distinction." His Barbera has won eight straight gold medals and it is one not to miss when visiting.

As mentioned, Ruthel is an accomplished artist and designer and has created more than 300 labels thus far, such as the striking rooster label for Rex-Goliath wines. And his artwork, along with that of many other local artisans, can be found and enjoyed inside the winery's tasting room.

FEATURED WINES: Italian varietals, including Barbera
TASTING COST: Complimentary
HOURS: Tuesday–Sunday, 11 AM–5 PM
LOCATION: 8032 South Main Street, Mokelumne Hill
PHONE: 209-286-1800
WEBSITE: www.frenchhill.com

MURPHYS

3 *Beaux Chevaux Tasting Gallery*

Murphy's newcomer Beaux Chevaux Tasting Gallery is not your standard tasting room. Owned by Mary Beth Davis and Nancy Morgan, Beaux Chevaux has something for the art lover, too. "We are the only tasting room and gallery combination in Calaveras County," said Davis, noting that the full-fledged gallery features

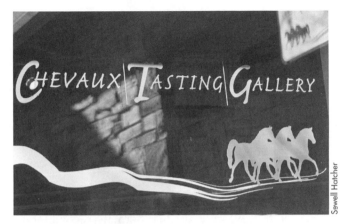

Sewell Hatcher

Sign greeting visitors to Beaux Chevaux

10 foothill artists currently on rotation. "That way, the designated drivers have something to do while their friends are tasting our wine."

Davis's amusing response is in keeping with the rest of her interview. "Nancy and I have been nuts about wine for most of our lives, and we decided to follow the lead of Mark Twain when he said, 'What work I have done I have done because it has been play. If it had been work I shouldn't have done it.'" The winery's name means "beautiful horses" in French, and Davis and Morgan owned three horses—Reggie, Zephyr, and Khia—when they were developing their logo. "My dad swears the first word I said was 'pony,'" smiled Davis. "We both grew up with horses, and Nancy even led trail rides for tourists in the Rocky Mountains when she was 11."

When asked about her winery background, Davis said: "I have been a banker for the last 20 years, and right now wineries are a lot more popular than banks, so I am glad to be opening our new business." Since Morgan is a working psychologist, she helps out in the winery and tasting room on the weekends. "One of us has to have a real job!" Davis exclaimed.

In 2008, Davis and Morgan purchased what many locals knew as the "Al Beckman" vineyard. Beckman planted it in the 1980s from scions taken from his father's Zinfandel vines in Lodi, which date back to about 1900. Next came the Syrah, then a second estate vineyard was planted in Zinfandel, Syrah, and at the request of Matt Hatcher of Hatcher Winery (see page 264), Cinsault was added five years ago.

"We make our wine with Matt [Hatcher] consulting and bailing us out when we run into trouble," said Davis. "We would not be open without his help. Matt and the other winemakers in Calaveras County have been super-supportive of us."

As Twain says, if it's work, then why do it? These fledgling winery owners have a lot of work ahead of them, but their playful attitude and outlook will see them through.

FEATURED WINE: Zinfandel
TASTING COST: Complimentary
HOURS: Friday–Sunday, 11 AM–5 PM
LOCATION: 466 Main Street, Murphys
PHONE: 209-728-1000
WEBSITE: www.bctastinggallery.com

4 *Black Sheep Winery*

The only black sheep in the Millier family is their winery, Black Sheep Winery. Much of the history of how Steve and Liz Millier got into the wine business can be found under the Milliaire Winery (see page 274). They acquired Black Sheep when longtime friends and winery owners David and Janis Olson decided to retire in 2007. The Olsons opened Black Sheep in 1984, and Steve helped them with their first crush. According to Liz, the Olsons lived on nearby Sheep Ranch and actually had sheep, including one black sheep, hence the name of their winery.

The matriarch of the Millier family, Liz oversees both the Black Sheep and Milliaire wineries. When asked if she was a winemaker, too—like her husband Steve and son Bob, the latter of whom is the winemaker for both family wineries—she laughed. "I'm a 'backseat' winemaker; I criticize often!" giggled Liz. She went on to explain that her role in this established winery family focuses on marketing and other required administrative duties. Someone has to hold down the fort!

Black Sheep's tasting room is located in a 150-year-old farmhouse at the east end of Main Street. The grounds are quaint and welcoming—you might even see a sheep or two grazing in the small grassy areas—and the inside is just as charming. Remember, these are Millier wines; you're guaranteed a great tasting experience every time!

One favorite and very popular Black Sheep wine is the True Frogs label, which has been around for many years. The label honors Calaveras County's annual Jumping Frog Jubilee. As Liz explained, "Dave [Olson] used to be a 'frog farmer' at Jumping Frog; he tended to the frogs underneath the stage."

Without a doubt, Black Sheep's popularity keeps the very knowledgeable and friendly tasting room staff jumping, including the couple's daughter and tasting room manager Kathy Millier. And we just can't resist ending with one of the wineries favorite lines, something you'll be sure to do after visiting Black Sheep: "Come baaaaaack soon!"

FEATURED WINE: Zinfandel
TASTING COST: Complimentary
HOURS: Daily, 11 AM–5 PM
LOCATION: 221 Main Street, Murphys
PHONE: 209-728-2157
WEBSITE: www.blacksheepwinery.com

---

5 *Bodega del Sur Winery*

One of the newer wineries in Murphys, Bodega del Sur Winery's goal is to help further a strong Spanish impression on this Irish namesake town. "We are giving our winery a Spanish touch," explained Evelyn Reyes-Umana, who owns the winery with her husband Victor. "Not only [do we have] a Spanish [winery] name, but our winemaker Chuck Hovey has vast experience in producing Spanish varietals like Tempranillo and Albariño. Moving forward, we plan to introduce many Spanish and South American varietals with local grapes that grow well in the foothills."

Located on Algiers Street near the famed Murphys Historic Hotel and Lodge, this small, appealing, charming winery draws one in. Upon entering, you'll be awed by the wrought iron light fixture that hangs from the center of the room. Reyes-Umana designed the light, which is blown glass in the shape of poppies, and commissioned an artist in Mexico to create it.

Girls' day out at Bodega del Sur

WINE MYTH } **You have to drink wine in a wine glass to enjoy it. Not true! In Italy, wine is enjoyed in regular glasses, and in Spain, you drink in leather wine boots (botas). Wine is a total experience, provided not only by the wine itself but by the food and the company. —Evelyn Reyes-Umana**

The winery's copper-clad bar sits atop what are known as "cocuchas," large ceramic jars made exclusively in the remote Purepecha Indian village of Cocucho, Mexico. According to the winery's website: "Each piece is hand formed without the use of a wheel, mold, or mechanical device. The colors and textures are unique and created when the artist uses a corn meal solution to splash on each piece before it is charcoal fired. The villagers were originally taught this method for making the pots more than 300 years ago . . . the pots were originally used for storing grain and water. Now they are pieces of art." And so is Bodega del Sur, a Spanish-rich treasure all its own.

FEATURED WINES: Spanish varietals such as Tempranillo
TASTING COST: $5 per person, applied toward a purchase or keep the glass
HOURS: Daily, 11:30 AM–5:30 PM
LOCATION: 457 Algiers Street, Murphys
PHONE: 209-728-9030
WEBSITE: www.bodegadelsur.com

6 *Brice Station Vintners*

Brice Station Vintners' brochures proclaim, "Altitude, Not Attitude." And do they have that right! At 3300 feet, the winery has one of the highest elevation vineyards in California. The drive to Brice Station is only 4 miles east of Murphys on Highway 4 but entails an elevation gain of 1000 feet; you'll soon see tall pines lining the highway. The winery's entrance on the left is announced via a bright red vintage pickup truck sporting a large sign in its bed; you can't miss it.

WINE MYTH } You need to know a lot about wine to enjoy it.
—Stuart Mast

Regarding attitude, there is absolutely no pretentiousness at this rustic winery. You are greeted with wonderful hospitality, like it must have been back in the 1800s when this site, then owned by the Brice family, was a popular stagecoach stop on the way to Calaveras Big Trees. Also found on the property is Quyle Kilns, the area's oldest family-owned and -operated production business. Both potters, founders Paul and the late Joyce Quyle started making their own clay formulas in 1941; they moved their pottery studio to this location in 1954. To this day, high-fired ceramics are on sale in their country-charm showroom, and you might even get to peek into the work area if they're not busy.

Brice Station Vintners's famed red truck and sign

The couple's daughter Pamela has taken over the kiln works, which produces more than 6,000 pieces a year, but patriarch Paul can sometimes be found throwing pots or teaching classes in the onsite blacksmith shop. (You can learn about them at www.quylekilns.com.)

Making pottery wasn't the only thing that fascinated this entreprencurial family. The Quyles' other daughter Dolores and her husband Stuart Mast decided in the 1990s to open a winery on the family's 100-acre property; the vineyard was planted in 1993 and the first wine produced in 2001. And you can definitely taste the mountain difference in their wine offerings; the Masts attribute the success of their vineyards to "a climate reminiscent of the Napa and Bordeaux regions [which have] in common a long summer pulse of warm days and cool nights." Their wine, served in a rustic barnlike structure, coupled with their self-proclaimed "unpredictable sense of humor," makes the drive up the hill worth the trip.

FEATURED WINES: Cabernet Franc, Merlot, and Cabernet Sauvignon
TASTING COST: Complimentary
HOURS: Tasting Room: Friday–Sunday, 12 PM–6 PM
HOURS: Quyle Kilns: Daily (except Tuesdays), 10 AM–5 PM
LOCATION: 3353 East Highway 4, Murphys
PHONE: 209-728-9893
WEBSITE: www.bricestation.com

---

7 *Domaine Becquet Winery*

A wine tasting trip to Main Street in Murphys would not be complete without a stop at Domaine Becquet Winery. Tucked into a small courtyard, the winery's tasting room is warm and inviting. Owners Roswitha and Charles Becquet de Mille are European—Roswitha is from East Germany, and Charles was born in California but was raised in France (his beautiful accent gives it away). Both have seen the world a zillion times over, but settled down in nearby Valley Springs, transforming an old building on their property into their winery. "The winery in Valley Springs was a

Roswitha and Charles Becquet de Mille

country inn during the Gold Rush and after, called 'Mountain Gate' since it was the gate to the mountains. Valley Springs was a dry town, but people could drink and dance where the winery is now located," smiled Charles.

The de Milles opened their winery, then the tasting room, many years ago in order to convince their children that their father was not in the CIA! For more on that story, read Charles's winemaker interview at **www.WineOhGuide.com.** For Charles, winemaking is part of his genetic makeup. "Our family has been in the wine business for five generations—Bordeaux originally [France]. And now, it's six generations with our son

Francois-Laurent." After his career as an international consultant, they wanted to start a winery in California. Their wines are made in the European tradition, "with less alcohol and less oak from the barrel. They are bottled by gravity and by hand," said Charles, who grew up in the vineyards of some of the best Bordeaux wineries in the world. "It's amazing to see the best in winemaking here and in Europe and do cross-fertilization of ideas and techniques."

WINE MYTH } Sweet wines are only dessert wines. In fact, some sweet wines are excellent with sauerkraut, blue cheese, or duck. **—Charles Becquet de Mille**

Visiting with Roswitha and her husband is an indulgence, especially if you enjoy learning about the culture of wine. "We explain a lot about the history of wine, the 'wine culture,' also the local culture since the Gold Rush. We offer an overview (when customers are interested) of the culture of wine and food worldwide," explained Charles. The two shared story after story with us, giggling and flirting with each other like a couple of love-struck schoolchildren, not a couple who have been married for more than four decades. They even playfully shushed each other in another language, much to our amusement.

There's even more to their history, specifically on Charles's side; he is a direct descendant of Thomas Becket of Canterbury. Back in the 12th century,

Thomas Becket was Archbishop of Canterbury and a supporter of England's King Henry II. Becket eventually went against Henry regarding the assets of the Catholic Church and was killed in England's Canterbury Cathedral in December 1170. The faithful throughout Europe recognized Becket as a martyr and in 1173, only three years after his death, he was canonized by Pope Alexander III.

Much has been written about this event in history, including *The Canterbury Tales* by Geoffrey Chaucer, which is about a group of pilgrims on their way to see the shrine of St. Thomas Becket; the Broadway production *Becket* in which Sir Laurence Olivier played the title role (Richard Burton played the equivalent in the film); and, more recently, Ken Follett's historical novel *The Pillars of the Earth*, which mirrors the story of Becket by way of a fictionalized accounting, with much based on the actual events leading up to Becket's assassination. "When [Becket] was murdered in the cathedral in December 1170, the family left England for the continent [Europe]. In 1919, my family came to California, but I was raised in Europe," Charles explained. To honor Becket, the winery uses the family coat-of-arms for their wine labels.

As mentioned, their tasting room is on Main Street, inside a small complex. They have a gift shop and a nice seating area in the courtyard. Their winery in Valley Springs is open during special events and by appointment only.

FEATURED WINES: Ports and a variety of European-style wines
TASTING COST: Complimentary
HOURS: Thursday–Monday, 11 AM–5 PM
LOCATION: 415-B Main Street, Murphys
PHONE: 209-728-8487
WEBSITE: www.becquetwinery.com

---

8 *Hatcher Winery*

Tucked away in the basement of the Old Segale Building is Hatcher Winery. A family name, the winery was a
longtime dream of Matthew Hatcher, who opened it in
2002. "Starting a winery looked like a great lifestyle,"
Hatcher explained when talking about his strong desire
to establish a winery. A single dad to his 6-year-old son
Sewell, Hatcher reflected on his decision to start the
business, "It's turned out to be a great lifestyle, but it's
certainly a lot more work than I ever imagined!"

WINE MYTH } When do you add the alcohol? —Matthew Hatcher

Family is an important aspect of this winery: Hatcher's brother, also named Sewell, is his business partner
and a professional photographer, as well. "Our dad's
name is Sewell, and tradition has it that the firstborn son
takes the name. Since [my brother] Sewell didn't have
any kids, we named my son Sewell." Confused yet? Well,

Sewell Hatcher

Matthew's son Sewell helps Dad with advertising!

don't be—while most wineries have wine cats and wine dogs (including this one, whose wine dog is a black Labrador retriever named Justin), Hatcher Winery goes one step beyond by having a wine kid! The young Sewell is his uncle's favorite model.

The building in which Hatcher Winery can be found has quite a history, one too interesting to dismiss. It was built in 1859 as a fireproof grocery and provisions store, and two years later it became a homestead then a bakery. Unfortunately, the baker accidentally shot himself and died when getting change for a little girl's $5 gold piece; he had rigged a gun in his cash drawer to shoot any would-be robbers. In 1871, the building was purchased by David Baratini and Paul Segale, the building's namesake. Segale and his wife raised their eight children in the building.

History aside, Hatcher, who is from this area, wears almost every hat in the winery, from owner to winemaker to salesman. "We like to think that we make good wine at a price that shows value. But I never would have thought that 40 to 50 percent of customers base their wine purchases on their experiences in the tasting room. That was something I've learned. You have to have great employees to make this happen." Hatcher and his group are active in the community and volunteer much time helping other start-up wineries in the area.

The mission at Hatcher is to do the best they can, and the word *compromise* isn't a part of their vocabulary. Their wines are wonderfully exquisite, their tasting room very welcoming, and their staff entertaining and engaging. And the place never fails to be packed to the rafters with wine lovers. Be it ever so humble—and delicious!

FEATURED WINE: Zinfandel
TASTING COST: Complimentary
HOURS: Summer, daily, 12 PM–5 PM; Winter, Thursday–Sunday, 12 PM–5 PM
LOCATION: 425-B Main Street, Murphys
PHONE: 209-605-7111
WEBSITE: www.hatcherwinery.com

9 *Indian Rock Vineyards*

Indian Rock Vineyards, a mile from downtown Murphys, has one of the most relaxing picnic areas in Calaveras County. Where else can you relax and enjoy a glass of wine surrounded by 70 acres of serene grounds and vineyards, including two picture-perfect lakes fed by 11 natural springs? And for the kid in you, owner Ed Bauer suggests feeding the large rainbow trout in the lake. What could be more fun?

WINE MYTH } The price of wine has no relationship to its quality.
—Ed Bauer

This beautiful valley has been home to many walks of life, and many forms of commerce, for tens of thousands of years. The Miwok wintered in the area, and the mortars, or grinding rocks, they used to prepare their meals can be found throughout the region. Trappers and adventurers were active in the region just prior to the Gold Rush in 1849. The property on which Indian Rock Vineyards now resides was turned into ranch land and owned by many different men until 1885, when Ethel Adams, a relative of Henry Adams (brother of President John Adams), purchased the property. Needless to say, in the U.S. in the late 19th century, it was rare for a woman to hold land. An avid outdoors enthusiast, Adams loved the area. She eventually started a dairy on the property,

Indian Rock's gorgeous grounds and tasting room

which operated for more than a half century, according to historian and author Judith Marvin.

"The dairy was known as Table Mountain Ranch Dairy," said Marvin, who was the director of the Calaveras County Museum for more than a decade. "I believe it closed in the 1940s or so." Marvin, who purchased Adams's home and has lived there for more than 30 years, has a wealth of photos and history on Adams, and other historians and major museums often consult her about Adams. You can see the house for yourself; it's the two-story house on the hill across the street from Indian Rock Vineyards.

Hailing back to its dairy days, Indian Rock's tasting room is the 1924 milking barn, beautifully redone to accommodate their winery and customers. You'll be awed by the striking open-beam construction with knotty-pine ceilings and the whimsical antlered chandeliers hanging throughout. And the gift area in the tasting room's entry way will tempt you to browse. But the highlight, of course, is the winery's "liquid" offerings; we particularly liked the Barbera and Petite Sirah. So if you're ready to relax, make the short drive to Indian Rock Vineyards.

FEATURED WINES: Barbera, Chardonnay, Vermentino, and Petite Sirah
TASTING COST: Complimentary
HOURS: Friday–Sunday, 12 PM–5 PM
LOCATION: 1154 Pennsylvania Gulch Road, Murphys
PHONE: 209-728-8514
WEBSITE: www.indianrockvineyards.com

---

10 *Ironstone Vineyards*

Undoubtedly, at 500,000 cases of wine sold annually, Ironstone Vineyards is the Sierra foothill's biggest wine producer. Ironstone is also a destination in and of itself, but thankfully it's not too "Napa-ish." Nobody snooty or snobby here, that's for sure, thanks to the Kautz family.

John and Gail Kautz started Ironstone in 1989. They were wine grape growers until 1988 when they decided, along with their four adult children, to create wine under their own label. They purchased 1,150 acres outside Murphys and began to dig into the mountainside, creating massive caves for wine storage. Steve Millier, Ironstone's winemaker and a winemaking legend in his own right, explains how the dual 85-foot-deep caves were created and describes his job at Ironstone in his winemaker interview (read about it at **www.WineOhGuide.com**). Millier owns a couple other wineries in the area: Black Sheep Winery (see page 253) and Milliaire Winery (see page 274). The miners who dug the Ironstone caves also named the winery. While blasting, they complained that the rock was like iron.

Built to resemble an 1800s gold stamp mill (where gold ore was processed), the winery building is seven stories tall counting the wine caves below. Their oak tasting bar, built in 1907 by the New Brunswick Bowling Ball Company in New York, was shipped around Cape Horn to its original location—A. J. Bumps Bar in the small California port town of Freeport. When the landmark closed in 1992, the bar was brought to Ironstone. Another famed antique at Ironstone is the historic Alhambra Theatre pipe organ (from Sacramento), which has been fully restored. The winery also features two gorgeous gift shops, a jewelry store, and an extensive art gallery. Then there's a state-of-the-art conference center and an outdoor amphitheater and entertainment complex that has hosted some of the

Winemaker Steve Millier (left) and co-author Ken
tour the famed caves.

biggest names in the entertainment world. To see those huge barrel-aging caverns for yourself, consider one of the daily tours.

Ironstone is one of the few wineries in the region to have its own executive chef, James Lehman. Actually, Ironstone has four chefs, with Lehman in charge. Lehman's culinary background is both impressive and vast. He oversees anything and everything epicurean at Ironstone, including cooking classes in the winery's gourmet kitchen, guest chef seminars, special events, and the winery's in-house gourmet delicatessen.

The grounds at Ironstone are absolutely amazing. With 14 acres of impeccably kept gardens, it is a picnicker's delight and a horticulturist's dream. In the spring, more than 300,000 daffodils bloom, with tulips, camellias, Dutch irises, rhododendrons, and azaleas following. Their grounds are so popular that Ironstone regularly updates a "flower watch" page on their website. And on weekends and special holidays, "Mario the miner" teaches visitors how to pan for gold at his miner's shack, located on the grounds next to the winery's gated entrance.

The winery's crowning jewel is the Kautz Crystalline Gold Specimen—a 44-pound crystalline gold piece. Discovered in nearby Jamestown in 1992, the gold is the largest specimen of its kind in the world, and the largest remaining piece of gold mined since the 1880s (larger pieces were found between 1849 and 1880, but none are known to exist today). Available for public viewing in the Ironstone Heritage Museum and surrounded by a high-security glass case inside a vault, the specimen is a thing of beauty and will take your breath away. Crystalline gold is the rarest form of gold, and the premium price can climb as high as $6,000 per ounce. Being the only one of its kind in the world makes the Kautz specimen priceless.

One of the most important aspects of Ironstone Vineyards is their employees, and that has a lot to do with the Kautzes and their philosophy of taking care of and treating their staff right. Considering all that must be accomplished each and every day at this enormous winery, one would think it would make a few of the employees grumpy. But we have yet to witness this. From the groundskeepers to the winery employees, from the tasting bar and gift shop gang to the administrative team, Ironstone's staff is genuinely happy, and it's the customers who reap the rewards by way of great service in a pleasing and relaxing environment. Bravo!

FEATURED WINE: Cabernet Franc (largest grower of varietal in the U.S.)
TASTING COST: Complimentary
HOURS: Summer, daily, 10 AM–6 PM; Winter, daily, 10 AM–5 PM
LOCATION: 1894 Six Mile Road, Murphys
PHONE: 209-728-1251
WEBSITE: www.ironstonevineyards.com

11 *Milliaire Winery*

Milliaire Winery, located in a converted gas station on Main Street in Murphys, is the namesake of one of the region's nicest guys and most prolific winemakers, Steve Millier. While both the winery and Millier's last name are pronounced the same (Mill-ee-air), there's a reason for the spelling difference: Since Millier was the winemaker for at least 10 different wineries prior to establishing his own, he didn't feel it was right to attach his name to a specific winery.

Milliaire means "milestone" in French, and the Millier family is known for many milestones. Besides Milliaire Winery, which is the oldest family-owned and -operated winery in Murphys, Millier and his wife Liz own Black Sheep Winery (see page 253), also found on Main Street. Their son Bob is the winemaker for both wineries, and daughter Kathy can be found running the show at Black Sheep. Millier, a sought-after wine consultant and expert, is also the head winemaker at Ironstone Vineyards (see page 269). For this family, the love of winemaking and Calaveras County go hand in hand. (To learn more about Millier, read his winemaker interview at **www.WineOhGuide.com**.)

After Millier received his enology degree in 1975, he took a job as winemaker at David Bruce Winery in Los Gatos. While at David Bruce, the couple desired to

Milliaire's tasting room with Jana Nadler behind the bar

establish their own winery by Millier's birthday, October 28 in 1983. And they did just that; Millier left David Bruce in 1983 and the couple opened Milliaire Winery in Murphys the same year.

But 1983 proved to be a tough year for the Milliers. Since they didn't grow any of their own grapes, they relied on other growers to provide the fruit. The 1983 harvest they had pre-purchased was ruined by early rains and their dreams were crushed. That was, until Frank Alviso of Clockspring Vineyards in Amador County called and asked the couple if they would be interested in some of his Cabernet Sauvignon grapes. They jumped at the chance. That fateful phone call and those grapes allowed the Milliers to open their winery by the end of 1983. And to this day, the winery still purchases their grapes from Clockspring Vineyards and also Ghirardelli Vineyards in western Calaveras County.

Milliaire Winery is housed in the town's former gas station and is affectionately referred to as the "Roadside Chateau." With its high ceilings, cement floors, and large bay doors, the converted station doubles perfectly as a winery, especially since Murphys Creek, found directly behind the building, provides natural air conditioning. According to Jana Nadler, Bob Millier's wife, "The building went through a couple of changes. It was a Phillips 66 gas station at one point in time (1969), then it changed to a Flying A gas station." When asked more about its history, Nadler said they didn't know much besides what an occasional customer who used to work there remembers. She added that they would love to learn more, and also would be thrilled to receive any gas station-related artifacts should anyone be generous enough to make a donation.

Most winery enthusiasts are familiar with the obligatory wine dog or wine cat, but Milliaire has a wine bird—Lefty, a female parrotlet. "Lefty was given to us by a friend of the family who couldn't house her anymore," said Nadler. Off in a corner of the tasting room, Lefty is a quiet bird, but as soon as you say "hello" to her, she welcomes you in full parrotlet chorus. She's a hit with young and old alike and is a fun addition to the Milliaire Winery family.

FEATURED WINE: Zinfandel
TASTING COST: Complimentary; large groups, busses, and limos,
$5 per person (refunded with purchase)
HOURS: Daily, 11 AM–5 PM
LOCATION: 276 Main Street, Murphys
PHONE: 209-728-1658
WEBSITE: www.milliairewinery.com

12 Muir's Legacy

Located in Murphys, Muir's Legacy is the namesake
of John Muir, one of the nation's most admired and
famous naturalists and conservationists. The winery is
owned and operated by his direct descendants, going
back six generations.

Much has been written by, and about, John Muir,
but you might be surprised by the winemaking angle.
Born in Scotland in 1838, Muir and his family immi-
grated to the U.S. in 1849. Twenty years later, Muir
traveled to California and fell in love with the Sierra
Nevada, especially Yosemite Valley. Through his writings and activism, Muir helped to preserve the valley as
a national park and to establish the national park system. Muir also founded the Sierra Club in 1892, serving as its president until his death in 1914.

Muir married Louie Strentzel in 1880, whose
family had a large ranch, including grapes (planted

Muir's Legacy wine label featuring John Muir, circa 1910

in 1853) in Martinez, California. Muir spent much of his time at the ranch. The couple had two daughters, Wanda and Helen. Wanda married Tom Hanna, and they had six children, including son John Muir Hanna. Hanna moved his family's ranch operation to Napa Valley in 1950 and quickly became known as a leader in the wine industry and in conservation and philanthropy as well. Hanna passed away in 2007, just shy of his 99th birthday. Keeping the Muir-Hanna winemaking legacy going strong, John's son Bill Hanna now manages the vineyards and grandson Michael Hanna, John Muir's great-great-grandson, is the winemaker. Visit the winery's website and you'll see little ones in a family photograph; these are Muir's great-great-great-grandchildren.

True to the senior Muir's legacy, the family farms sustainably and organically, celebrating "with every vintage the respect and connection that John Muir had with the glories of nature." And according to the family, a portion of the profits go toward conservation concerns.

While the wine is made at the Muir-Hanna Vineyards in Napa, the winery's only tasting room is in Murphys, right where John Muir would most likely have wanted it—in his beloved Sierra Nevada. Located near the corner of Big Trees Road and Main Street, the tasting room is elegant. The winery's staff is friendly and accommodating, and their knowledge of the wine and family history is commendable.

The winery is noted for its Chardonnay, which is an anomaly considering that Chardonnay grapes aren't typically grown in this appellation. But since the wines are made in Napa, and tasted in Murphys, white wine lovers can rejoice! And the deep and delicious Merlots are just as good; you can enjoy both varietals, and many more offerings, while browsing the old photos and memorabilia of Muir in the tasting room.

One fun note shared by tasting room manager Steven Gomez is that Muir's Legacy wines are featured at Yosemite National Park stores. "Everything we do at our winery is grounded in the ideals that John Muir set," explained Gomez. If John Muir was still with us today, he would, without a doubt, be very proud of his family's legacy.

FEATURED WINES: Chardonnay and Merlot
TASTING COST: Free
HOURS: Daily, 11 AM–5 PM
LOCATION: 219 Main Street, Murphys
PHONE: 209-728-0500
WEBSITE: www.muirslegacy.com

13 *Newsome-Harlow Winery*

Newsome-Harlow Winery is a fun stop on your downtown Murphys wine escape. The elegant tasting room and contemporary court-yard, complete with stylish sofas and a swanky motif, offers a respite to enjoy their artisan wines and gourmet food pairings.

According to winery owner and winemaker Scott Klann, Newsome-Harlow is a family name. "My original partner's last name was Skenfield, and mine was Klann . . . you can't call yourself 'Klann-Skenfield,'" They decided to use their mother's surnames: Newsome on Klann's side and Harlow on Skenfield's side.

WINE MYTH } **Wine is serious. —Scott Klann**

The winery's choice of names, such as Donner Party and El Portal, honor California legacies and landmarks, while others, like their dessert wine The Dash and their full-bodied red Train Wreck, have more auspicious be-ginnings. "'Train Wreck' was what I was calling two lots of wines I wasn't happy with. They were much better to-gether then they were on their own. So I called it 'Train Wreck' as a working title until I came up with something better, but it ended up sticking," explained Klann.

While their wine is made just outside of town, their food is created on-site in their state-of-the-art

Newsome-Harlow's elegant and inviting courtyard

gourmet kitchen. This is where you'll find the other half of Newsome-Harlow—Chef Melanie Klann (and yes, she's also Scott's wife). When asked about working with a member of the family, Klann said, "Looking forward to ending every day *not* sleeping on the couch."

The winery strongly supports sustainable agriculture. When asked what he felt was the most important, albeit misunderstood, aspect of sustainable agriculture, Scott Klann responded: "That each different piece of land requires a different set of viticultural practices in order to be sustainable. It is not a specific set of rules, it is a philosophy that must adapt to each different piece of land where it is applied."

FEATURED WINE: Zinfandel
TASTING COST: Check website
HOURS: Monday–Thursday, 12 PM–5 PM; Friday–Sunday, 11 AM–5:30 PM
LOCATION: 403 Main Street, Murphys
PHONE: 209-728-9817
WEBSITE: www.nhvino.com

14 Solomon Wine Company

Solomon Wine Company opened its doors in 2002. While they make their wines in Fair Play and Clarksburg, their tasting room is located on Main Street in what used to be Murphys's firehouse. "We still have a working siren to summon volunteer firemen, or wake up the whole county, if needed," said Rich Boone, a principal shareholder in the company. The winery has only set off the siren twice, first accidentally (they didn't know what the switch was for) and the second time during one of the town's event weekends.

WINE MYTH } **There is a right wine to pair with the right food.**
—Rich Boone

But this eclectic and delightful winery doesn't need to use a siren to draw attention to their tasting room, as it's a popular stop for wine lovers. Their success is evident by the three different brands they

The swanky, expansive tasting room at Solomon

offer: Cloud 9, the elegant cornerstone of Solomon; Garsa, the winery's Mediterranean-centric homage to the Sierra foothills; and last, Muse, according to its label, a "bright and playful and mostly irreverent— but certainly not irrelevant" wine.

Although many of the tasting rooms found in Murphys are small, Solomon's used to be a firehouse, and the sheer size of the room is a delight. It's fun and refreshing, from the dual and curvy tasting counters to the wit and humor of the staff (they obviously enjoy their work!). "We don't take our wine too seriously, and we don't take ourselves too seriously. I don't know anyone else who features mixed drinks made with their wine. Basically, you never know what you're going to get in the tasting room, but it's almost guaranteed to be different from the time before," said Boone.

Solomon Wines was named after King Solomon. "Solomon was the wisest king, hence Solomon wines are the 'wise choice,'" Boone explained, sharing that he often dresses up in full costume as the Biblical figure, as well as other assorted characters, to the delight of tasting room customers.

And with Murphys Community Park less than a block away, the staff at Solomon can create (for a fee) a special picnic basket, featuring their wine and foodstuff from the deli next door. They also have a second tasting room at the Old Sugar Mill in Clarksburg; check their website for directions and hours.

FEATURED WINES: Zinfandel, Syrah, Mediterranean varietals, and proprietary blends
TASTING COST: $3 per person, refunded with purchase
HOURS: Summer/fall, daily, 1 PM–5 PM; off-season, check website
LOCATION: 397 A Main Street, Murphys
PHONE: 209-728-8290
WEBSITE: www.solomonwine.com

15 *Tanner Vineyards*

Located at the very busy four-way stop of Main Street and Big Trees Road, Tanner Vineyards can be easy to overlook. But that would be tragic, as this very young winery is deserving of its place on Murphys' Winery Row.

Even though Tanner Vineyards opened their doors in 2008, the family winemaking history goes back generations. According to owner Nanette Tanner, her great-grandfather, Angelo Sciaccaluga, came to this region from Genoa, Italy, in the 1860s. Settling near Vallecito, he made wine and brandy and was the first winemaker in Calaveras County to pay an alcohol tax. The townspeople of Vallecito had such a hard time pronouncing her great grandfather's last name that they called him "Pyshon" instead, after a place in his homeland. The family was so well regarded that, when it came to naming streets, the road near where he and his family lived was named "Pyshon Lane."

WINE MYTH } **Table grapes are much sweeter than wine grapes.**
—Nanette Tanner

Fast-forward nearly 150 years and today four generations of the Tanner family are carrying on the tradition of their ancestors. While it shares a building with a barber and small gift shop, Tanner's tasting room is inviting from the outside, with its white picket fence and

Courtesy of Tanner Vineyards

Inviting front porch at Tanner's tasting room

corner courtyard. Inside, seasoned barn wood can be found throughout, along with an array of century-old tools used by this agricultural family. And the family's strong ties to Calaveras County can be seen in the numerous black-and-white photographs that hang in the tasting room, including one of Sciaccaluga pouring wine on the porch of this Vallecito winery in the late 1800s. "When our customers come into the Tanner Vineyards tasting room, we want them to get a sense of who we are and where we come from," explained Tanner.

Tanner Vineyards's flagship wine is a 2004 Mélange de Mère, dedicated to Tanner's mother, Jacqueline Rose. And surprisingly, despite the vineyard's youthfulness, their wine is very good. Tanner's winemaker, Scott Klann, owner of Newsome-Harlow Wines (see page 281) on Main Street, has helped the family realize their dreams. "He knows our vineyards inside and out; its soils, its trellising design, the volcanic rock deposits, the airflow and light weather patterns . . . he is all about the vineyard," explained Tanner.

Without a doubt, this young winery will enjoy a very long life in Murphys, thanks to a little help from family and friends, past and present.

FEATURED WINE: Syrah
TASTING COST: Complimentary
HOURS: Monday–Friday, 1 PM–5 PM; Saturday, 12 PM–5:30 PM; Sunday, 12 PM–4 PM; off-season, check website
LOCATION: 202 Main Street, Murphys
PHONE: 209-728-8229
WEBSITE: www.tannervineyards.com

16 *Vina Moda Winery*

In Italian, *vina moda* means "vine style." And that is what you'll get when you visit Vina Moda Winery—style. Kirsten and Nathan Vader are the owners of Vina Moda. Kirsten comes from an Italian family where drinking two bottles of wine a day was commonplace. When the couple decided to open a winery, Kirsten got to choose the name because of her heritage. Nathan's one smart guy! And it's obvious upon entering Vina Moda who does what. Nathan is the winemaker, and Kirsten, the interior decorator and the glue that holds the place together. Nathan's story of how he got into winemaking, and some of the interesting approaches he employs, including playing his harmonica to the wine as it ferments and ages and his talents as a "wine whisperer," is discussed at length in his winemaker interview at **www.WineOhGuide.com.**

Kirsten's area of expertise is her sense of style. The historical stone building that houses Vina Moda's tasting room originally belonged to an Italian cobbler during the 1800s. Kirsten and Nathan's remodel of the old building is stunning. Before the couple was married in 2002 and Kirsten began working at the winery full-time, she worked at an interior design firm, and it shows. From the exposed plaster and stone to the enchanting wall behind the bar—complete with copper patina tiles, 125-year-old rough-sawn barn wood, and antique Indian doors from the 1700s—to the unique furniture and the special touches throughout, her stroke of design genius is apparent. But her style is most evident in the winery's tasting bar; upon entering their tasting room, you'll be awestruck by the face of the bar, which is covered in hundreds of glistening peacock eyes. With mirrored copper tile that looks as if it has just seen a spring rain and the hidden vine that crawls across their distinctive label, the bar is anchored by baroque black glass chandeliers that hang opulently above. "I wanted the whole tasting room to be as balanced and enchanting as our wines," smiles Kirsten. "We had such an amazing canvas to begin with, and Nathan's carpentry skills really made it all possible."

This boutique winery brings a lot to their community. They offer their facility and beautiful backyard for myriad local events, including a welcoming picnic spot. During these events or when visiting their tasting room, you'll probably meet the rest of the Vader family: Shaolin, a floppy-eared Doberman pinscher, and Dali Lala, a dachshund with the markings of a Doberman. The only difference between their comical mirror images is their size. Just like their "people," both wine dogs are friendly, outgoing, curious, and fun to be around.

Vina Moda Winery is at the four-way stop of Main Street and Big Trees Road. Look for the enchanting little white stone building—you can't miss it.

FEATURED WINES: Cabernet Sauvignon, Viognier, and Barbera
TASTING COST: $3
HOURS: Saturdays, 12 PM–6 PM
LOCATION: 147 Main Street, Murphys
PHONE: 209-728-1917
WEBSITE: www.vinamoda.com

17 *Zucca Mountain Vineyards*

"Wines for every season and adventure" is the theme at Zucca Mountain Vineyards. Located on Main Street in Murphys, Zucca Mountain's tasting room occupies a portion of the Old Fisk Building. Built in 1859 by Freeman Dunbar, the building was originally a saloon then a bowling alley, followed by a general store, post office, drug store, public library, and a tonsorial (beauty) parlor. Zucca is spread out over three different stories of the building. The Cellar, which is the main tasting room, is the most fun, but watch your head as the doorway is low! While partaking in some wonderful wines, you can enjoy the inviting coolness of the cellar, along with some regional history. The second level, the Piemonte Room, is an attractive gift shop, and the third level, known as the Toscana Room, doubles as an additional tasting room on busy weekends.

Owners Carol and Gary Zucca were home winemakers before going commercial in 1996. Prior to

Basement entrance to Zucca Mountain's tasting room

establishing the business, Carol, a biologist with a bio-chemistry background, taught for most of her career. Her husband Gary, a Vietnam vet and former naval officer with a Ph.D. in sociology and organizational behavior, teaches college in addition to overseeing the production aspects of the operation. Carol said that there is always something to learn and enjoy when it comes to the wine business: "We are bilingual (English and Spanish) and are working on our Italian. We attend conferences abroad to exchange cultural ideas and winemaking practices."

Their wine is made off-premises where their vineyards are located, on a peninsula at the New Melones Reservoir. This location has a unique microclimate with cooling breezes from the lake that moderate the temperature and provide an excellent environment for Rhone and Italian varietal grapes. And the entire family is involved in the business: son Matt is an engineer, Michelle (Matt's wife) is a marketing expert, son Tony is a molecular biologist, and Carol's brother Darrell and his wife Kathy cater special events and design innovative equipment for the winery.

Something that's different from the other wineries in the area, and a treat we definitely enjoyed, is the complimentary food samplings Zucca Mountain offers. The Zuccas encourage food and wine pairings by holding a monthly contest, open to the public. Submit your recipe, paired specifically with one of their wines, and you could win two bottles of Zucca Mountain wine!

More information, along with recipes of past winners, can be found on their website.

FEATURED WINES: Barbera and Syrah Port
TASTING COST: Complimentary
HOURS: Daily, 12 PM–5 PM
LOCATION: 425-E Main Street, Murphys
PHONE: 209-736-2949
WEBSITE: www.zuccawines.com

VALLECITO

18 *Laraine Winery*

Just a few miles south of Murphys is the town of Vallecito, home of Laraine Winery (formerly Gerber Vineyards). Owners Laraine and David Gerber are not originally from these parts. Established Hollywood icons (David, a producer, and Laraine, an actress under the last name of "Stephens"), the couple spent their getaway time in Murphys. In the 1960s, David, who has produced or executive produced notable shows like *Police Woman* and *Walking Tall,* bought the historic Murphys Hotel and Lodge with some of his University of the Pacific college buddies. Twenty years later, David used the area as the location for one of his many television series, *Seven Brides*

Laraine's tasting room resembles a quaint country home.

for Seven Brothers. During production of that show, the couple purchased a beautiful historic estate in an isolated valley just outside of town. It was then that Laraine caught the winemaking bug and educated herself on the business through much research and also courses at the University of California at Davis. In the early 1990s, the first fruit was harvested, with the first wine released in 1993 to great acclaim. Fifteen years later, the winery continues to produce high-end estate wine.

The winery is named, of course, after Laraine, who has starred and guest starred in hundreds of roles in movies and television shows including *Barnaby Jones, The Love Boat, The Mod Squad,* and *Vega$.* When asked what he looked forward to almost every day when it came to working with a family member, David explained, "We enjoy the beauty on our doorstep and working toward a common goal."

At an elevation of 1800 feet, the vineyard that surrounds the winery boasts 10 different estate-grown varietals. The fruit is of such high quality that it has been purchased by other wineries, including renowned Carneros Creek and Stag's Leap. Winemaker John Gibson, a veteran of Napa Valley, nurtures the vineyard like a loving father and over the last decade has created some amazing wines. His philosophy on making wine can be found at the winery's website; he comments on the finished product: "My greatest joy is to be able to open a new vintage of Laraine wine with friends and family and with each sip taste that unmistakable Sierra foothill signature."

Visiting the winery is a refreshing break from the hustle and bustle of winery hopping in downtown Murphys. And don't become discouraged if you wonder, "Where in the world is the winery?" while driving down Six Mile Road—it's only a mile from Highway 4, so you'll get there soon enough. Coming into the valley, you'll see a barn and an 1880s cream-colored house nestled under two large trees; the house is the tasting room. From the winery's very accommodating staff to the amazing wines, from the inviting picnic area to the scenic backdrop, Laraine is worth discovering. And who knows, with a Hollywood producer as the owner, you might even be "discovered," too!

FEATURED WINES: Sangiovese, Cabernet Sauvignon, and Syrah
TASTING COST: Complimentary
HOURS: Friday–Sunday, 11 AM–5 PM
LOCATION: 3675 Six Mile Road, Vallecito
PHONE: 209-736-4766
WEBSITE: www.larainewinery.com

---

19 *Twisted Oak Winery*

Why did the chicken cross the road? To partake in some Twisted Oak wine. You don't believe us? Okay, we'll rephrase the question: Why did the chicken walk up a long and gently winding gravel road, through the Rubber Chicken National Forest, laughing at all the hilarious signs posted along the way, to the very top of a small mountain with gorgeous views and the site of a 300-plus-year-old twisted California blue oak? Again, to partake in some Twisted Oak wine. Seriously!

If you have a sense of adventure *and* a sense of humor, then get your fanny to Twisted Oak Winery! You might not make it to the summit, however, because you'll keel over from laughter along the way. Every few tenths of a mile, small Burma Shave–style billboards are posted, along with a very silly assortment of rubber chicken "crypto-graphic" signs.

The twisted **tasting room at Twisted Oak!**

The brilliantly mad mind behind all this craziness is winery owner Jeffrey Stai, who obviously has a thing for rubber chickens and the sublime: "We tend to take ourselves a little less seriously, but we do take the wine seriously, and I think our scores of awards reflect that, not to mention that they're delicious—the wines, not the awards. We're trying to do something special with varietals that seem to do very well here but are not well known, mostly from Spain, like Tempranillo, Garnacha, and Graciano."

Because the winery is built on a hillside, Stai uses old-world gravity flow techniques, allowing for gentle movement of the grapes, juice, and wine through the winemaking process and down to barrels in the winery's 4,200-square-foot wine cave.

The Twisted Few is the name of the Twisted Oak's wine club, apropos considering all the amusement the group enjoys. For example, once a year the winery holds a "pirate party" for members, even though they encourage members to dress like "naughty pirates" whenever they visit. And the club even has their own page on the winery's website and can get their fix of everything twisted via the winery's blog page, where "El Jefe" himself, as Stai is called, posts his thoughts (www.elbloggotorcido.com).

WINE MYTH } Spitting wine is wasting wine. I do try to encourage our customers to pace themselves while tasting. And I always encourage them to spit—that's not wasting, it's tasting! So many customers think it's wasteful, and unfortunately too many wine people encourage that idea. **—Jeff Stai**

Twisted Oak Winery's delicious wine is so popular that they offer a second tasting room in the heart of downtown Murphys, in the childhood home of Albert Micheloon, the first U.S. citizen to win a Nobel Prize in physics. He emigrated from Poland with his family in 1848 in search of gold, but his father owned and operated a store. Stai picks up the story from there: "Albert later became a physicist and discovered the speed of light . . . he actually measured it to such a sufficient accuracy that it gave Einstein an idea."

Today, the historic home is charming from the outside, but within are the infamous rubber chickens and

some amazing wine. Now you know why the chicken crossed the road, and you should follow it to Twisted Oak Winery!

FEATURED WINES: Spanish-style blends, Rhone-style wines, and varietal wines
TASTING COST: Complimentary
PHONE: 209-736-9080
WEBSITE: www.twistedoak.com

MAIN TASTING ROOM
HOURS: Daily, 10:30 AM–5:30 PM
LOCATION: 4280 Red Hill Road, Vallecito

SECONDARY TASTING ROOM
HOURS: Vary
LOCATION: 350 Main Street, Murphys

+ More Area Wineries

MURPHYS

Broll Mountain Vineyards
HOURS: Saturday and Sunday, 1 PM–5 PM
LOCATION: 106 Main Street, Murphys
PHONE: 209-728-9750
WEBSITE: www.brollmountainvineyards.com

Chiarella Wines
HOURS: Friday–Sunday (and holiday Mondays), 12 PM–5 PM
LOCATION: 431 Main Street, Murphys
PHONE: 209-728-8318
WEBSITE: www.chiarellawines.com

Frog's Tooth Vineyards
HOURS: Friday, 1 PM–5 PM, Saturday and Sunday, 11 AM–5 PM
LOCATION: 380 Main Street, Suite 5, Murphys
PHONE: 209-728-2700
WEBSITE: www.frogstooth.com

Lavender Ridge Vineyard
HOURS: Daily, 11 AM–5 PM
LOCATION: 425-A Main Street, Murphys
PHONE: 209-728-2441
WEBSITE: www.lavenderridgevineyard.com

Stevenot Winery Tasting Room
HOURS: Check website
LOCATION: 458 Main Street, Murphys
PHONE: 209-728-0148
WEBSITE: www.stevenotwinery.com

SIDE TRIPS

There are two things that most people who travel to Calaveras County want to see. First there are the big trees, those giant sequoias at **Calaveras Big Trees State Park** (www.parks.ca.gov). Although Native Americans had been familiar with these ancient giants, it wasn't until 1852 that Augustus T. Dowd "discovered" the North Grove of giant sequoias. It quickly became a tourist attraction and has remained so since Dowd's day. An easy trail meanders through the North Grove, even taking you through the huge, centuries-old, walk-through sequoia that was hollowed out by fire. The park's South Grove has a longer hiking trail.

The second thing that most people think about when visiting this area is the famous **Angel's Camp** frog jumping contest. Inspired by Mark Twain's story "The Celebrated Jumping Frog of Calaveras County," the annual **Frog Jumping Jubilee** (www.frogtown.org) brings thousands of people to the fairgrounds for this fun event each May. Twain's first published story was about Jim Smiley and his frog Dan'l Webster and Jim's attempt to win a bet about whose frog could jump the farthest. While competitors' frogs are not likely to be loaded down with lead shot at today's competitions, the antics practiced by frog owners to get their green amphibians to jump can be quite hilarious. Don't own a frog? Loaners are available.

For Mark Twain fans, immediately outside Angel's Camp is a replica of the **Mark Twain Cabin,** the small structure that the famous author occupied during his visit to the Angels Camp area. It is here where Twain penned his story about jumping frogs. The cabin belonged to the Gillis brothers— Twain merely visited for a while. The original cabin burned, but one of the Gillis brothers identified the site, and a replica cabin was constructed in 1922. The cabin sits atop **Jackass Hill,** a short-lived Gold Rush hot spot, a mile off Highway 49. Even though road signs identify the turnoff, it's a steep drive to the top, so please watch your speed as the narrow road winds through a country residential area.

If you want to visit the Irish Queen of the Sierra, head to **Murphys.** The town was named for Daniel and John Murphy, who settled here in 1848. Smart businessmen and shrewd traders, the Irish brothers made their fortune supplying the miners. It is said they were millionaires by the time they reached age 25. The reason the town doesn't have an apostrophe in its name is because, at first, the brothers each wanted to own the town and name it after himself. This led to a bloody fistfight, which caused both brothers to tumble into a 30-foot-deep pit. They had to work together to get out and learned the importance of cooperation. The Murphy brothers decided that neither of them would own the town, but they would share in the name instead.

With all the many wonderful shops, restaurants, and wineries found on the Murphys main drag, be sure to stop at **Murphys Historic Hotel and Lodge.** Built in 1856, the hotel has hosted the likes of General Ulysses S. Grant, Horatio Alger, and Mark Twain. Even the notorious outlaw Black Bart whetted his whistle at the hotel's famed and supposedly haunted bar, which is still open to the public after all these years.

Just outside of Murphys in **Vallecito** is **Moaning Cavern** (www.caverntours.com). The guided tour takes you down 234 stairs, 165 feet below the surface. Nearby in **Mountain Ranch** is **California Cavern** (www.caverntours.com), the state's earliest known cave to offer tours. Opening in 1850, it was originally called Mammoth Cave due to its size. During the hot summer months, trips into both caves, where the temperature stays at about 55°F, are welcome treats.

SIDE TRIPS

For More Information

Calaveras Winegrape Alliance
P.O. Box 2492
Murphys, CA 95247
866-806-WINE (9463) or 209-728-9467
www.calaveraswines.org

Calaveras Visitors Bureau
P.O. Box 637
1192 South Main Street
Angels Camp, CA 95222
800-225-3764 or 209-736-0049
www.gocalaveras.com

CalaverasGROWN
P.O. Box 2101
San Andreas, CA 95249
www.calaverasgrown.org

Acknowledgments

When we started this book, nearly every one of our friends, and even more of our family members (no, we're not all winos!), volunteered to help us with our research. While only a few actually accompanied us during our travels, we are deeply indebted to those who, with much love and patience, supported our latest writing adventure.

Because our family endured the brunt of our research escapades, we must thank them first:

To Dahlynn's 12-year-old son Shawn, who joined us on a few trips and helped with the photography and collecting brochures. He also was a real trooper when it came to meeting deadlines; having grown up in the writing business, Shawn knows the drill and, thankfully, also knows his way around a kitchen. You're the best, big guy!

To Ken's adult son Jason and his family—wife Anna and children Ashlyn and Jacob: We really missed watching the grandkiddos, but with another book out of the way, we're now free to spoil them rotten!

To Dahlynn's sister Shayla Seay, a budding photographer and the person who kept us pointed in the right direction for the last few months. Once again you have gone above and beyond the call of duty, and we love you for it. You're the best sister, best sister-in-law, and best friend anyone could ever want!

To Dahlynn's parents Cliff and Scharre Johnson: Thanks for sending all of the newspaper clippings on anything and everything having to do with wine. We love you dearly and are thrilled to dedicate this first *Wine-Oh! Guide* to you both.

Next, thank you to our wonderful neighbors who are always happy to help out: To Bill Falkenstein for his love and support when it came to feeding our two pooches while we were on the road: It's wonderful knowing that the doggies were well cared for and loved. To Ken and Michele Cemo, who tagged along with us one day when we researched both Nevada City and Grass Valley: We had a blast exploring this region with you both, and can't thank you enough for playing navigator, being our gofers during interviews with winemakers, and for also buying lunch—you can join us anytime! To Jim and Nikki Garner: Thanks for keeping an eye on our home while we were away doing research, which was quite often for this book! And to Sue and Jeff Feather: A hardy "cheers!" for coming over and helping us drink a few bottles of the wine we received as gifts from wineries. Good thing you live within walking distance!

And, of course, a big thank you is in order for the entire gang at Wilderness Press, including associate publisher extraordinaire Roslyn Bullas and editor Laura Shauger. Thank you for your faith and for entrusting us to pen yet another book for you. We truly appreciate your openness in considering titles and ideas that are new to Wilderness Press, and, as promised, we will continue to make you look good! And our invitation is still open to join us for a day of wine tasting (tell them you're doing research).

This book wouldn't be possible without all the expertise and support from the many wonderful winery owners, winemakers, and grape growers we interviewed during our research. While we may have accidentally left a few people out of this section, please know it wasn't on purpose, and that we can't thank you enough for imparting your knowledge to our readers:

To Anna Davies, the executive director of the Calaveras Winegrape Alliance: *Wow* is the only word to describe your commitment to this project. Without you and your help in getting wineries to complete their surveys in minute detail, the Calaveras chapter would not be as strong and wonderful as it turned out. We'll hire you anytime!

To Jolaine Collins of Collins Communications, and also the media contact for El Dorado Winery Association: Thank you so much for your help and guidance in navigating the nearly 50 wineries in your region.

To Jamie Lubenko, the executive director of the Amador Vintners' Association: Your dedication to the town of Plymouth and the county's vintners is commendable, and we appreciate your help.

To Vicky Morris, owner of Secret Ravine Vineyard and also our contact for the Placer County Wine and Grape Association: Thanks for your help and expertise!

To the staff of the Northern Sierra Wine Country association: Thanks for your help and support.

To historian Judith Marvin of Foothill Resources: Thank you for helping us with Calaveras County history. We learned a lot!

To Mike Owens, owner of Crystal Basin Cellars and also the "head dude" of the newly formed Carson Road Wineries Association: Thanks for your kindness and support of our book.

To Bill Easton, owner of Terre Rouge and Easton wineries: A very warm thank you for providing us with maps of the Sierra foothills appellation and other necessary documents, all of which proved valuable in deciding our book's direction and focus.

To Anne and Phil Starr of Sierra Starr Vineyards: Thank you for your guidance when it came to contacting wineries in Nevada County.

To author Eric Costa, whose historical writings were extremely valuable in explaining the history of the wine regions: Thank you and good luck with your new book *Gold and Wine: A History of Winemaking in El Dorado County*. Anyone who wants to order a copy can contact him at costa@volcano.net.

To Rosemary Bluhm of C. G. Di Arie: Thank you for your insightfulness, guidance, and indispensable "insider knowledge" on the best ways to wade through the political waters of some of the wine regions. We owe you big time!

To the gang at Bray Vineyards—namely Stephanie Anderson, Robin Bray, and John Hoddy—thanks so much for imparting your knowledge and wisdom, but more so for reminding us to laugh!

And our biggest thank you of all goes to the gang at Dobra Zemlja, especially co-owner Mike Daugherty, co-owner Milan Matulich and his wife Victoria, and Norina and Jeff Johnson. It was here that the *Wine-Oh! Guide* idea came to be. While picking up our monthly wine club shipment, we were chatting with Norina about our other travel books and how for us, traveling the world is a business expense. It was then that Dahlynn posed the question, "Why don't we pen a story about Dobra and then write off today's trip?" Her idea snowballed from there and the book was born. And Dobra continued their support with Milan granting us our first winemaker interview and photo shoot, which we included as part of our book proposal. We tease Milan that his toothy grin—under that signature mustache of his—along with his shaggy hair, summertime bare feet, pink tutu, and wonderful outlook on life, got us the book deal. Salute, friends!

Index

A

Alger, Horatio 305
Amador Cellars 168, 174–176
Amador Council of Tourism
 241
Amador County 169–241
 Barbera 182, 185, 190, 195,
  197, 199, 230
 Cabernet Franc 174
 Cabernet Sauvignon 216,
  228
 Chardonnay 204
 Mission 204
 Petite Sirah 174, 185, 199
 Pinotage 234, 236
 Pinot Grigio 233
 Port 193, 207
 Primitivo 174, 182, 195
 Sangiovese 179, 182, 185,
  197, 233
 Sauvignon Blanc 230
 Syrah 174, 197, 224, 225,
  230
 Verdelho 185
 Vermentino 182
 Viognier 216
 White Zinfandel 120, 121,
 Zinfandel 169, 171, 174,
  176, 179, 182, 188, 191,
  193, 195, 196, 197, 201,
  202, 205, 207, 208, 211,
  212, 213, 214, 219, 220,

 222, 223, 225, 228, 230,
  233, 234
Amador County Chamber of
 Commerce 241
Amador Foothill Winery 168,
 177–179
Amador, Jose Maria 169
Amador Vintners' Association
 241, 310
Apple Hill 85, 90, 166
Apple Hill Growers Associa-
 tion 167
Argonaut Mine 240
Auburn-Foresthill Bridge
 69
Auriga Wine Cellars 159
Avanguardia Wines 39
Avio Vineyards 168, 231–233

B

Bantam Cellars 168, 180–182,
 201
Barbera 6
Barkley Historic Homestead
 Winery 160
Baumbach Wines 46, 49–52
Beaux Chevaux Tasting Gallery
 242, 250–252
Black Chasm Cavern 240
Black Sheep Winery 242,
 253–255, 270, 274
Boa Vista Orchards 162

313

Bodega del Sur Winery 242,
    255–257
Boeger Winery 72, 74, 116,
    119–123, 132
Bordeaux 6, 84, 95, 115, 209,
    259, 261, 262
Bray Vineyards 168, 182–185
Brice Station Vintners 242,
    258–260
Broll Mountain Vineyards 301
Busby Cellars 72, 149–151

C
C. G. Di Arie 168, 185–188
Cabernet Franc 6
Cabernet Sauvignon 6, 7
Calaveras Big Trees State Park
    244, 258, 303
Calaveras County 243–306
    Barbera 250, 269, 294
    Cabernet 280
    Cabernet Franc 260, 273
    Cabernet Sauvignon 260,
        275, 280, 291, 297
    Chardonnay 247, 269, 280
    Cinsault 252
    Merlot 260
    Petite Sirah 269
    Port 264, 294
    Sangiovese 297
    Syrah 247, 252, 285, 288,
        294, 297
    Tempranillo 255, 257,
        298
    Vermentino 269
    Zinfandel 252, 255, 266,
        277, 283, 285
Calaveras Visitors Bureau 306
Calaveras Winegrape Alliance
    306, 310

CalaverasGROWN 306
California Cavern 305
Cantiga Wineworks 72,
    152–155
Carson Road Wineries Associa-
    tion 167, 311
Chana, Claude 47, 48, 68
Chardonnay 11
Chateau Routon 161
Chatom Vineyards 126, 242,
    246–247
Chaw'se Regional Indian
    Museum 239
Chevalier Winery 72, 145
Chiarella Wines 301
Clos du Lac Cellars 237
Colibri Ridge Winery and
    Vineyard 72, 91–93
Coloma 2, 73, 96, 97, 127,
    165, 239, 248
Coloma Cemetery 127
Cooper Vineyards 168,
    188–190
Coufos Cellars 40
Crljenak Kastelanski 6
Crystal Basin Cellars 72,
    75–77, 311

D
D'Agostini, Enrico 212, 213
David Girard Vineyards 72,
    124–127
Davis, John A. 191
Davis, Joseph 191
Deaver Vineyards 63, 168,
    191–193
Dillian Wines 168, 194–195
dkcellars 72, 93–96
Dobra Zemlja Winery 168,
    195–197, 312

Domaine Becquet Winery 242,
    260–264
Dono dal Cielo Vineyard 46,
    62–64
Double Oak Vineyards and
    Winery 39
Drytown Cellars 237

E
El Dorado County 73–167
    Barbera 84, 93, 103, 104,
        112, 118, 119, 121, 123,
        157, 158
    Cabernet 147, 148
    Cabernet Franc 77, 84, 87,
        103, 115, 119
    Cabernet Sauvignon 84, 95,
        96, 103, 135, 147
    Chardonnay 155, 158
    Counoise 133
    Gewürztraminer 87, 131
    Grenache 127, 134, 140, 143
    Malbec 103
    Merlot 74, 84, 103, 104,
        111, 115, 121, 147, 148
    Mourvèdre 77, 97, 127, 134,
        140, 143
    Muscat 101
    Petite Sirah 101, 103, 105,
        106, 115, 136, 137
    Pinot Noir 79, 80, 81, 114
    Port 77, 84, 93, 101, 118,
        140, 158
    Primitivo 93, 103, 114, 115
    Rhone 6, 75, 124, 131, 132,
        133, 140, 142, 143, 144,
        155, 179, 208, 224, 293,
        300
    Rose 111, 131
    Roussanne 143
    Sangiovese 83, 103, 131
    Sauvignon Blanc 104, 107,
        109
    Syrah 97, 106, 111, 127,
        132, 140, 143, 144
    Tempranillo 114, 115
    Viognier 88, 97, 98, 106,
        127, 134, 143, 144
    Zinfandel 74, 87, 95, 96,
        98, 101, 103, 105, 106,
        107, 112, 114, 115, 118,
        119, 122, 123, 149, 151,
        155, 158
El Dorado County Farm Trails
    Association 167
El Dorado County Historical
    Museum 166
El Dorado County Visitors
    Authority 167
El Dorado Winery Association
    167, 310
Empire Mine State Historic
    Park 15, 16, 43

F
Fair Play Winery Association
    167
Fenton Herriott Vineyards 72,
    128–131
Findleton Estate and Winery
    72, 78–81
Fitzpatrick Winery and Lodge
    160
Fleur de Lys Winery 72,
    96–98
Fossati Vineyard 120, 121
French Hill Winery 242,
    248–250
Frog Jumping Jubilee 244, 303
Frog's Tooth Vineyards 301

G

Garnet Sun Winery 159
Gold Bug Park and Mine 165
Gold Hill Vineyard 162
Grandpère Zinfandel 205, 207
Granite Springs Winery 72,
    99–101, 118
Grant, Ulysses S. 305
Grass Valley/Nevada County
    Chamber of Commerce 44
Griffith Quarry Museum 69

H

Hangtown 164, 165
Hatcher Winery 242, 252,
    264–266
Haraszthy, Agoston 4
Holly's Hill Vineyards 72,
    131–134

I

Idaho-Maryland Mine 15
Illuminare Estate 159
Indian Grinding Rock State
    Historic Park 170, 239
Indian Rock Vineyards 242,
    267–269
Indian Springs Vineyards 14,
    29–31
Ironstone Vineyards 242,
    269–273, 274
Iverson Vineyards and Winery
    72, 102–104

J

Jackass Hill 244, 304
Jeff Runquist Wines 168,
    198–199
Jodar Vineyards and Winery
    72, 82–84

K

Karly Wines 168, 180, 181,
    200–202
Karmère Vineyards and Winery
    237
Kennedy Mine 170, 240

L

Laraine Winery 242, 294–297
Latcham Vineyards 72, 99,
    115–119
Lava Cap Winery 72, 134–137
Lavender Ridge Vineyard 302
Lombardo-Fossati Home 74,
    120
Lombardo, Giovanni 121
Lone Buffalo Vineyards 46,
    53–55
Lucchesi Vineyards and Winery
    14, 21–23

M

Madroña Vineyards 72, 85–87
Maidu 239
Malakoff Diggins State Historic
    Park 16, 41
Marshall Gold Discovery State
    Historic Park 126, 165
Marshall, James 73, 124, 165
Merlot 6, 7, 11
Milliaire Winery 242, 253,
    270, 274–277
Miners Foundry Cultural
    Center 32, 42
Mission grapes 4, 47, 60, 120,
    202, 217
Miwok 170, 171, 239, 267
Moaning Cavern 305
Montoliva Vineyard and
    Winery 14, 18–21

Moraga, Gabriel 243
Mount Aukum Winery 162
Mt. Vernon Winery 46,
    55–57
Muir's Legacy 242, 277–280
Murphy, Daniel 244, 304
Murphy, John 244, 304
Murphys Historic Hotel and
    Lodge 255, 294, 305
Murrieta, Joaquin 248
MV Winery–Miller Vineyards
    160

N

Naggiar Vineyards and Winery
    39
Narrow Gate Vineyards 72,
    138–140
Nevada City Chamber of
    Commerce 44
Nevada City Winery 14, 32–35
Nevada County 15–44
    Barbera 25, 31
    Cabernet 23
    Cabernet Franc 23, 31, 35
    Cabernet Sauvignon 23, 28
    Chardonnay 23
    Merlot 28
    Petit Verdot 35
    Port 29
    Sangiovese 20, 21, 25
    Sauvignon Blanc 28, 29
    Syrah 31, 35, 38
    Viognier 38, 291
    Zinfandel 23, 29, 35
Nevada County Narrow Gauge
    Railroad Museum 42
Newsome-Harlow Winery
    242, 281–283
Nichelini Winery 119, 123

Nine Gables Vineyard and
    Winery 168, 202–204
North Bloomfield 41
North Star Mine 15
North Star Power House 43
Northern Sierra Wine Country
    44

O

Oakstone Winery 161
Old Town Auburn 68
Ophir Wines 46, 64–66

P

ParaVi Vineyards 159
Pelton Wheel Mining Exhibit 43
Perry Creek Winery 72,
    105–106
Pilot Peak Vineyard and
    Winery 14, 36–38
Pinot Grigio 6
Placer County 47–70
    Aglianico 50, 52
    Barbera 52, 57, 60
    Cabernet 57
    Cabernet Sauvignon 61
    Charbono 50, 52
    Chardonnay 87
    Grenache 55
    Mourvèdre 55, 60
    Nebbiolo 50
    Petite Sirah 53
    Sangiovese 60, 61, 62,
    Sauvignon Blanc 60, 62
    Shiraz 56
    Syrah 55, 57, 58, 59, 60, 66
    Tempranillo 58, 59
    Zinfandel 48, 52, 57, 59, 60,
        62, 63, 64
Placer County Courthouse 68

Placer County Museum 68
Placer County Wine and Grape
    Association 70, 311
Placer Valley Tourism 70
Priest Mine 165
Primitivo 6
Prohibition 4, 5, 33, 74, 120,
    171, 212, 220

R
Rancho Roble Vineyards
    67
Reagan, Ronald 74, 121
Renwood Winery 168,
    205–208
Roberts, George 15

S
Sangiovese 6
Secret Ravine Vineyard and
    Winery 46, 60–62, 311
Serra, Father Junipero 3, 4
Shadow Ranch Vineyard and
    Winery 72, 107–109
Shenandoah Vineyards 168,
    209–211, 212
Sierra Knolls Vineyard and
    Winery 14, 24–25
Sierra Oaks Estates 72,
    110–112
Sierra Starr Vineyard 14,
    26–29, 311
Sierra Vista Vineyards and
    Winery 72, 141–144
Single Leaf Vineyards 161
Sobon Estate 168, 171, 209,
    212–214
Solomon Wine Company 242,
    283–285
Solune Winery 39

Stevenot Winery Tasting Room
    302
Stonehouse Vineyards and
    Winery 168, 215–216
Stone's Throw Winery 160
Story Winery 168, 217–219
Sutter Creek Wine Tasting 238
Sutter Gold Mine 240
Sutter Ridge Vineyards and
    Winery 168, 191,
    234–236
Syrah 6

T
Tanis Vineyards 168, 172–174
Tanner Vineyards 242,
    286–288
Terra d'Oro Winery 168,
    220–223
Terre Rouge and Easton Wines
    168, 223–225, 311
TKC Vineyards 168, 226–228
Toogood Estate Winery 72,
    113–115
Twain, Mark 243, 251, 303,
    304, 305
    cabin 304
Twisted Oak Winery 242,
    297–300

U
Uhlinger, Adam 171, 212, 213
Ursa Vineyards 160

V
Van der Vijver Estate Winery
    161
Venezio Vineyards and Winery
    162
Viña Castellano 46, 58–59

Vina Moda Winery 242,
    289–291
Vina Noceto 238
Viognier 6, 11
Volstead National Prohibition
    Act 4

W
Wakamatsu Tea and Silk Farm
    Colony 127
White House 121
White Zinfandel 6
Wilderotter Vineyard and
    Winery 168, 229–230

Windwalker Vineyard and
    Winery 72, 132,
    156–158
Winery by the Creek 161
Wofford Acres Vineyards 72,
    88–90

Y
Young's Vineyards 238

Z
Zinfandel 6, 7
Zucca Mountain Vineyards
    242, 291–294

About the Authors

Together, authors Ken and Dahlynn McKowen have 50-plus years of professional writing, editing, publication, marketing, and public relations experience. They have had more than 2,000 articles, stories, and photographs published, and are authors or coauthors of  *Chicken Soup for the Entrepreneur's Soul; Chicken Soup for the Soul in Menopause; Highroad Guide to the California Coast;* national award-winner *Best of California's Missions, Mansions, and Museums;* and *Best of Oregon and Washington's Mansions, Museums, and More.*

They own Publishing Syndicate (www.Publishing Syndicate.com), which provides writing and editing services for publishers. They also release a free monthly writing and publication e-newsletter for new and established writers and offer for sale several e-books relating to the craft of writing and getting published.

When they're not traveling the world, the McKowens reside near Sacramento, California, where they spend their free time volunteering at their local elementary school and in the evenings, enjoying an occasional glass of foothill wine.